MOVING BASES

ROYAL NAVY MAINTENANCE
CARRIERS & MONABS

MOVING BASES
ROYAL NAVY MAINTENANCE
CARRIERS & MONABS

By
Commander David Hobbs MBE Royal Navy

**Essex County
Council Libraries**

Foreword

by
Dr David M Stevens
Director Strategic and Historical Studies
Sea Power Centre - Australia

In the uncertain security environment of the early 21st century many western nations appear to be rediscovering the need for an expeditionary strategy; if only because it makes more sense to deal with threats to your national interests on someone else's shore rather than your own. The difficulty comes when attempts are made to match resources to intentions and, striving to maintain strategic relevance, even the armed services of mid-ranking powers have increasingly laid claim to the mantle of an expeditionary force. But fielding such a complex capability requires more than a simple name change, and it remains to be seen whether equipment and structures will be acquired that possesses sufficient flexibility to operate for prolonged periods at a distance from permanently established bases. Too often, when prioritising the ratio of 'tooth to tail' in a force, policy makers focus on the hardware, and the less glamorous logistics and maintenance 'tail' comes off second best. Moreover, since all expeditionary operations will involve at least some cooperation with allies it is worth remembering that coalitions work best when partners bring with them everything they need.

To navies the issues of reach and sustainability are hardly new, for they have always been used as a tool to project power and influence well beyond national borders. The Royal Navy in particular has a long and honourable role in the maintenance of Great Britain's widespread maritime interests, and the British Pacific Fleet offers one of the most interesting examples of the expeditionary use of naval power. But while much attention has been paid by historians to the cut and thrust of BPF operations, remarkably little has been written on the firm foundations that allowed them to occur.

In "Moving Bases", David Hobbs contributes to the redress of this imbalance in a manner that can accurately be described as groundbreaking. He has not only produced a fascinating book on the wartime workings of the Fleet Air Arm, but also offers us a welcome reminder of the huge effort that must always go on behind the front lines. He describes in great detail, for example, the ships and organisation that went to make up 'the air train', a hitherto largely neglected aspect of the BPF's support operations. No reader could fail to be impressed by the sheer scale of the establishment required to maintain the striking power embodied in five armoured fleet carriers, three light fleet carriers and seven escort carriers across the vastness of the Pacific. Yet it is also food for thought that this fleet, fielded by a navy at the height of its wartime strength, could not operate entirely alone. Subordinate to the US Navy in a command sense, and including contributions from Canada, New Zealand and Australia, the officers and men of the BPF could nevertheless take pride in the fact that they were able to take the fight to the heart of the enemy; fighting side by side with the Americans as professional equals.

The ultimate success of the BPF is a tribute to the flexibility of maritime air power and the ingenuity and perseverance of many thousands of nameless men and women. David Hobbs has written a book fully worthy of their memory.

Canberra 2007

In memory of my friend David Brown who gave me the original idea from which this book grew.

Introduction

The use of depot ships to maintain destroyers and submarines grew throughout the first half of the twentieth century. The concept of the mobile, tented airfield evolved during the First World War. Faced with the need to provide engineering support for carrier-borne aircraft in a war in the Pacific, 12,000 miles away from the United Kingdom, the Admiralty made use of both ideas to support the air groups in the operational carriers during the Second World War and after. Similar ideas were used in the Korean War.

By August 1945, three maintenance carriers, several aircraft component repair ships, a Transportable Aircraft Maintenance Yard (TAMY) and ten Mobile Operational Naval Air Base (MONAB) had been commissioned. Between them, they provided over 1,000 naval aircraft for the British Pacific Fleet in its operations against Japan. They did much more, of course, including the provision of 'home bases' for the squadrons to disembark to in Australia. When the war was over they had to destroy aircraft in large numbers, dumping many in sea off the east coast of Australia.

In this book I tell their story for the first time in print. The work serves as an introduction to the Fleet Air Arm's many achievements behind the 'front line' in the Pacific Theatre. There is always more detail but, as the Second World War passes beyond living experience, I hope I am not too late to pay tribute to the men who achieved a great deal. May their memory never fade.

David Hobbs
Twyford
2007

Acknowledgements

I am, as always, grateful to my wife Jandy for her help with research and to my son Andrew for his unfailing support for everything I do.

Jan Keohane and Catherine Rounsfell of the Fleet Air Arm Museum Archive who gave a great deal of help. Their continuing support has been of great value to me throughout the time that it has taken to put this work together.

The majority of the images are from my own collection, built up over years of research and many of which were inherited from the late David Brown, Head of the Naval Historical Branch. I am grateful to the Royal Australian Navy for permission to use images which have been annotated accordingly and to the Fleet Air Arm Museum which gave permission for the images of the interior of *HMS Unicorn* and the steam catapult trials in *HMS Perseus* to be used.

Printed and bound by J. H. Haynes & Co. Ltd., Sparkford

Contents

Chapter One

THE CREATION OF AN AIR LOGISTICS ORGANISATION FOR THE BRITISH PACIFIC FLEET

After the absorption of the RNAS into the embryonic RAF in 1918, the Admiralty lost control of aircraft procurement and the logistic support for the fleets deployed throughout the world. Between the two world wars, aircraft carriers operated from base ports and relied on RAF logistic arrangements to provide repair facilities and replacement aircraft. Once the Admiralty assumed full administrative control of the Fleet Air Arm from 1937 it began to build up its own repair and maintenance organisation to fulfil storage, deep maintenance and repair tasks. RN Aircraft Yards were established at Donibristle and a number of other places but such was the scale of expansion during the Second World War that continued support was needed from RAF Maintenance Units. This shore based infrastructure worked in the Atlantic and Mediterranean Theatres but after the rapid Japanese expansion of 1941/42; British bases at Singapore and Hong Kong in the Far East were captured. The Pacific campaign was fought over vast distances with mobile maritime forces and whilst main bases ashore were important, the US Navy demonstrated the imperative need for mobile support units to sustain fast carrier task forces in action. No equivalent British structure existed with the result that, when the British Government announced that the Royal Navy was to deploy a fleet to the Pacific to fight alongside the Americans, a logistic support force had to be created from scratch. It would need to be built up from within the Navy's own resources with no certainty of outside help.

Staff forecasts of the British forces to be deployed to the Pacific varied enormously in the early months of 1944. At one stage six Army divisions, eighty-seven RAF squadrons and a large naval force were proposed but the impossibility of moving and supporting such a force caused estimates to be reduced. The allied leaders finally agreed at their Ottawa Conference in October 1944 that only a reduced British Pacific Fleet (BPF) would be deployed. This was to comprise four or five fleet aircraft carriers, about ten escort carriers, two battleships, five cruisers and destroyer flotillas. A second carrier striking force with the new light fleet carriers was to be deployed as the ships were completed. It was assumed that the war would continue into 1946 and, possibly, well into 1947 so that logistic support would need to be created to support the expanding BPF throughout that period. Even the reduced fleet would need very considerable backing both ashore and afloat if it was to undertake prolonged operations at sea on the extensive scale by then common practice in the US Navy without frequent resource to harbour facilities. Failure to provide logistic support on an adequate scale meant that Admiral King, Chief of US Naval Operations, would regard the fleet as a drain on his own Pacific Fleet's resources and refuse to accept it.

Admiralty planners had begun to study the problem of maintaining a modern fleet containing an aircraft carrier striking force in 1936. They studied scenarios where fleet bases were lost, unavailable, damaged by enemy action or far distant from the operational areas. Their ideas were put into sharp focus in 1943 when the concept of a BPF was first mooted and the need for a Fleet Train on similar lines to the one deployed by the USN was accepted. In consequence a mission under Admiral C. S. Daniel was sent to the USA, the US Pacific Fleet Headquarters in Hawaii and Australia in early 1944 tasked with examining the US organisation in detail. It was made clear to him that the Royal Navy would have to provide its own ships, make its own supply and repair arrangements and be self-sustaining with regard to naval, armament, victualling and air stores. It would also have to provide its own

furnace fuel oil (FFO) and aviation gasoline (AVGAS). With regard to most stores this was logical since British weapons and equipment were incompatible with American stock. Ironically, by 1945 the Fleet Air Arm's front line contained more American than British types but these had been so extensively modified that they differed to a very large extent from the USN standard and they, too, were incompatible. Generously, the USN did offer Admiral Daniel a share in any excess facility it had ashore and afloat in the combat area and to allow British use of its forward-deployed port facilities. It was prepared to help make good emergency or temporary battle damage repairs to British ships on an identical basis to its own units. Lodger facilities for British carrier-borne aircraft would be provided at any airfield under USN control adjacent to a fleet anchorage but the Americans would not repair, maintain or replace British aircraft. These concessions were most helpful and were almost always exceeded when the two fleets joined forces in 1945.

Detailed planning began in May 1944 when the

Implacable and ***Victorious*** *alongside during a replenishment period in Sydney. A third fleet carrier can be seen in the Captain Cook Dry Dock in the top right of the picture.*

British Naval Liaison Party arrived in Australia. It comprised Admiral Daniel and just three staff officers and, at the time, they had no clear idea when the fleet would arrive or even precisely where it was to operate. By the time approval for the formation of the British Pacific Fleet was given, however, Admiral Daniel's team had produced a detailed overall administration plan. This two hundred and fifty page document was revised in detail by a committee known as the Joint Administration Planning Sub Committee (JAPSC) of the Australian Defence Committee (ADC). This body assessed the cost of effort in terms of the manpower and materials that would be demanded of the Australian Government to achieve the Admiralty's aim. An overriding consideration was the acute shortage of manpower and this meant that new commitments could only be met by the re-allocation of existing men from other tasks. Fortunately several American contracts were due to lapse in early 1945, making real estate and manpower available.

The document produced by the Sub Committee was entitled "*Potentialities of Australia as a Base for Royal Navy Forces*"; JAPSC 1/44 dated 20 November 1944. This formed the basis for the development of a main fleet base with its supporting naval air stations throughout 1945. Several changes were made to it in 1945 for various local and strategic reasons.

The appointment of Vice Admiral (Q) (VA (Q)) was established on 10 November 1944 with responsibility for the logistical support of the whole BPF. The implementation of the air plan devised by the planners devolved onto the air section of his staff, which was based in Melbourne. On 28 December 1944 Flag Officer Naval Air Stations (Australia) (FONAS (A)) set up his headquarters in Sydney. His title was later changed to Flag Officer Naval Aviation Pacific (FONAP) and, for the sake of continuity, the later title will be used. From the nature of his appointment he assumed responsibility for the detailed planning of the development of air facilities both ashore and afloat. Inevitably, the fact that the two headquarters were not co-located led to some difficulties between planning and execution during 1945 but these were gradually overcome.

FONAP was responsible to VA (Q) for the adminis-

tration of all air establishments serving the BPF and for air logistical arrangements under three main headings:

- The supply of aircrews, aircraft and aero-engines up to and including the forward areas.
- The supply of information to enable the correct provisioning and distribution of other air material.
- The maintenance and repair of aircraft beyond the capacity of the Fleet Air Maintenance Group (FAMG).

Further, he was responsible to the Commander-in-Chief BPF for arrangements to receive disembarked squadrons from the fleet carriers and for the training of aircrew to meet the Fleet's requirements.

VA (Q)'s air staff was too small to carry the whole responsibility for planning the expansion of air facilities to meet the BPF's rapidly growing requirements. At first this involved the simultaneous development of five, eventually growing to twelve, air establishments. It comprised a Commander (P) who acted as an assistant chief of staff for air matters. Working for him were two Air Engineer Officers (AEOs), a Lieutenant Commander for air planning and organisation and another for airfield layout and planning. The latter had a Third Officer WRNS and a draughtsman to assist him. As a consequence, FONAP's staff had to take on the work of planning. The plans were then passed on to VA (Q)'s staff for arrangements to be made for their execution with the relevant Australian Service.

Even before the first ships of the fleet arrived in Australian waters FONAP's staff had to deal with four widely different activities. These were:

a) Planning.
b) Administration.
c) Air logistics.
d) Advice to the C-in-C BPF on technical air matters and, in the absence of ACS 1, on air operational matters.

Planning alone covered the development of twelve large air establishments from small beginnings into large naval air stations and administration covered all

the functions carried out by the Admiral (Air) and his large staff in the UK. The field of logistics was a new one, the extent of which continually expanded as the Pacific War progressed. It did not prove possible to divide the staff into sections to work on these activities individually; in consequence all staff officers had to cover all requirements and the strain was heavy. Increases in staff numbers were planned to take place as officers became available after the end of the war in Europe but, in the event, few arrived before VJ Day.

On his arrival in Australia, Admiral Sir Bruce Fraser the C-in-C BPF set up his headquarters temporarily in Sydney. It was his original intention to move into a forward headquarters in due course, following the example of Admiral Nimitz, the C-in-C US Pacific Fleet, who set up a forward HQ in Guam. Had this move taken place, the logistic planning including the setting up of intermediate and forward bases and support for the BPF would have been left in the hands of VA (Q) and FONAP. These two authorities would have to work in the closest co-operation but were situated 450 miles apart. A Review was carried out to see if it was possible to separate that part of FONAP's organisation, which must stay in Sydney from that element which should work alongside VA (Q) in Melbourne. The conclusion was reached that air stations should be administered by a Commodore Naval Air Stations with a headquarters in Sydney and that FONAP should move to Melbourne with staff to accomplish the overall policy control, planning and logistics functions. In the event, the C-in-C never moved to a forward headquarters and FONAP remained in Sydney with his staff of about 110 officers, WRNS officers and warrant officers. The Commodore's appointment was cancelled. Although separation from the staff of VA (Q) was not ideal, in truth it did not seriously effect the problems of supporting Fleet Air Arm Units in the Pacific. Rather, the biggest difficulties were found to be in the area of airfield procurement and development. Experience showed that Sydney was the correct place for FONAP staff, giving them the opportunity to carry out urgent and close consultation with carriers arriving on station and returning between operations.

Early in 1945, it was intended that forward logistical control would be exercised from an intermediate base. The Philippines were proposed as a suitable strategic location and it was intended to establish six RN Air Stations there, including one equipped as a Receipt and Despatch Unit (RDU). A Commodore Forward Naval Air Stations acting as the logistic agent of FONAP in Australia would have administered these. San Pedro Bay in Leyte Gulf was actually used by the BPF for replenishment in April 1945 during the Okinawa Campaign but there were no facilities ashore and the Fleet Aircraft Maintenance Group (FAMG) met the carriers' needs for replacement aircraft. It gradually became clear, however, that no intermediate base could be set up in the Philippines in time to support the operations of the BPF off Japan and the plans were eventually cancelled.

This change of plan led to a re-evaluation of logistic control in the forward area. The key unit of the FAMG during Operation "Iceberg" had been *Unicorn* which had lain in Leyte Gulf between 23 March and 22 May 1945. Her commanding officer Captain H.G. Merewether, an Australian serving in the RN, fulfilled the duty of Forward Area Aircraft Co-ordinating Authority. This involved the complicated matters of distributing aircrews and aircraft, co-ordinating and meeting as far as was possible the requirements of individual carriers and keeping FONAP informed of new replacements required. He was assisted by Commodore W.P. Carne RN, the Commodore Commanding 30th Aircraft Carrier Squadron (ACS 30) in *Striker*. This system had proved broadly successful and so it was decided to improve on it by appointing the commanding officer of *Pioneer*, which had recently joined the BPF, as Commodore Air Train (COMAT) flying his broad pendant in *Pioneer*. He was given the necessary staff and a Directive, which is reproduced at the end of this chapter. This laid out, clearly, the logistical and administrative chains from FONAP, through COMAT to the carriers and from the C-in-C through RAFT. This organisation worked well in the short period that elapsed before the war ended. Consideration was given to proposals to create an organisation along the lines of the USN COMAIR Pacific, which would have been entirely responsible for the air logistic support of the fleet. It would have

None of the shore establishments were complete when taken over - RNAS Schofields in February 1945.

had direct control over all the replenishment and ferry carriers and of the shipping required to move air material. This system would have had the advantage of centralisation of responsibility, organisation and control and would have, undoubtedly simplified the whole process. However, in 1945 the Royal Navy could not have assembled the necessary resources, especially staff officers, required and the necessary radical changes in the material and stores supply organisations would have been difficult to accomplish in wartime.

On the whole, the BPF air organisation worked adequately, given the resources available to it. In the conditions that prevailed in Australia in 1945, it is difficult to imagine an alternative that would have worked any better.

AIR ENGINEERING

Unlike other warships, aircraft carriers operate a weapons system - aircraft - that are technically more complex than the parent vessel itself. The need to maintain aircraft has always influenced the carrier's ability to generate sorties to meet its required task. Maintenance falls into two categories, planned and unplanned.

Planned maintenance in 1945 included daily inspections, before and after flight inspections and "mainchecks" at set numbers of flying hours. Engineers attempted to even out the major servicing events so that they did not all fall at once since this would make excessive demands on manpower and "ground" the squadron until the work was complete.

Most engines and components were "lifed" by set numbers of flying hours and had to be replaced by new or refurbished items at the major inspections. It would be a judgement decision whether or not to replace items that were not yet life-expired in an airframe that was already stripped down for other work in order to save time and manpower later. This would assume that sufficient spares were available to cover the "lost" hours caused by early replacement and this was seldom the case in the BPF.

Unplanned maintenance included the repair or replacement of failed or battle damaged components and airframe structure. Before a period of sustained operations, engineers in fleet carriers would try to clear as much major servicing as possible to have resources available for unplanned work. This would also have the benefit of giving the squadron the maximum number of aircraft to fill the flying programme.

The composition of the flying programme was of fundamental importance. When the Illustrious class fleet carriers were designed, they were to have an air group of only 36 aircraft which would be flown off in small numbers thoughout the day. These were to locate the enemy fleet, shadow it, slow it with a modest torpedo attack and spot the fall of shot of the battleships' guns in action. Replacement aircraft in the repair carrier *Unicorn* were to be close at hand. Reality by 1945 was very different. Air group size had grown to 54 in the early ships of the class and over 80 in the last two units. Many of these were kept in a large deck park and there was insufficient room for them all to be struck down into the hangar, even for shelter or major component changes. The requirement to launch regular fighter CAPs and Anti-submarine patrols still existed but the over-riding requirement was the deck load strike. This was a "pulse" of power

Aircraft ferried in "less than ideal conditions" from the UK.

intended to attack the enemy at sea or on land with the maximum number of aircraft. Routine, hour-based maintenance was possible in the earlier method but extremely difficult in the latter. Thus aircraft that could not be maintained, inspected or repaired overnight to be ready for the dawn deck load strike were very much a "waste of space". In the worst cases, they were stripped of useful components and literally pushed over the side. The increase in the size of the air group meant, under the squadron maintainer system, that many more sailors had to be embarked but there were still not enough to get the task done once aircraft "clocked up" the need for hours-based inspection and maintenance work. Accommodation in the fleet carriers was cramped and primitive and, without air conditioning, was barely tolerable in the tropics. The wastage of aircraft that were recoverable, given better maintenance facilities may seem profligate today but the USN worked a very similar system at the time and made less attempt than the British to return "duds" to maintenance yards where they could be refurbished. The effect of this in both navies was an increasing demand for new and refurbished aircraft and, in the case of the BPF, bigger and more efficient aircraft erection and storage facilities were needed in Australia.

In addition to the maintenance problems, flying propeller-driven aircraft from straight deck carriers was a dangerous business and operational losses were common even without contact with the enemy. In the Pacific, carriers could expect to lose up to 20% of their aircraft in any given operation. These added to the requirement for a constant stream of new and refurbished aircraft to keep them at operational efficiency and their provision was the purpose behind the maintenance carriers and MONABs.

In order to understand the efforts made to support the aircraft embarked in the BPF, it is necessary to put Air Engineering commitments of the air logistic support organisation into context. In Australia and the Pacific these fell broadly into three disciplines:

- The erection and preparation of new aircraft for front line service.
- The maintenance and repair of aircraft and components.
- Assistance to disembarked squadrons for maintenance and repair work beyond their own capacity.

Of these, erection proved to be by far the largest commitment and, had the war continued longer than it did, the needs of the fleet could not have been met by this source alone. Maintenance and repair would need to have assumed considerably more importance in order to make up the difference. The magnitude of the problem of providing the fleet with serviceable aircraft in the necessary numbers had been considerably under-estimated by the planners in the UK. During the period from 1 March to 15 August 1945 a total of 730 aircraft were passed into service with the BPF. The average number of man/hours needed to render serviceable aircraft that had been shipped to Australia varied but the following examples give some idea of the task.

An Avenger, delivered erect in a ferry carrier, took about 1800 man/hours to be prepared for operational service. A Firefly, delivered onto Sydney Docks dismantled in crates having been transported stowed in a merchant ship, took about 2,000 man/hours to prepare. A Hellcat, which had arrived partially erected and coated in "Erenol" preservative, took about 1,000 man/hours. An Avenger, similarly coated took about 2,250 man/hours. The figures for man/hours are for ratings' overall time on duty, not just the time worked on the aircraft and include such activities as Divisions, Sick Parades, Defaulters and Men-Under-Punishment musters. The aircraft coated in "Erenol" were far more likely to be in good condition than other aircraft ferried into the theatre. Crated aircraft were generally in reasonable condition but required more work to prepare and the large components were difficult to handle, given the shortage of cranes available within the BPF. The aircraft that had been ferried erect on the flight decks of escort carriers were, generally, in poor condition. Although the majority of these had very few flying hours, many had spent prolonged periods in storage in less than ideal conditions in the UK, India and Ceylon. Further, the methods used to preserve them were often inadequate, particularly those shipped

direct from the UK. In consequence, a great deal of work had to be carried out on these to render them fit for operational service.

Throughout 1945 the work of erection was made even more difficult by the severe shortage of spare components, tools and equipment. There was also a general shortage of cranes, trestles, jacks and other ground equipment, particularly in the first few months but the problem persisted throughout 1945. The short-term solution was to rob components from aircraft awaiting erection in order to complete the urgent commitments in hand. Robbing obviously reduced the number of airframes available for preparation but it also increased the workload on the erection teams and made it difficult to set up production lines that flowed smoothly. One of the many lessons learnt by the MONAB organisation in Australia was that erection could only satisfactorily be carried out in a properly equipped shore establishment with ample hangarage equipped with overhead lifting gear and workshops. The establishment must also have access to a well-equipped all-weather airfield for the test flying of aircraft as they came off the production line. It is unlikely that MONAB 7, equipped only with two small Dorland portable hangars and supported only by a Mobile Maintenance (MM) Unit, would ever have produced a satisfactory output from a forward airfield had it been required to do so. RN Air Station Bankstown on the other hand was taken over from the RAAF with hangars, workshops and hardstandings appropriate to the MR task. Its airfield, however, was unsatisfactory in that it was dusty in summer and muddy in winter. Thus aircraft that had been prepared to operational standard could often not be test flown immediately and output suffered.

The transport of aircraft ashore in Australia was another important area that was underestimated by the planners. Again taking Bankstown as an example, aircraft that arrived in Sydney docks had to be taken to the airfield 14 miles away and, once erected, towed back for embarkation in a ferry carrier for onward shipment to the fleet, a 28 mile round trip. More than half of this was through heavily built-up Sydney suburbs. This was a considerable undertaking and the Royal Navy's facilities would have been inadequate to

deal with it. Fortunately, the RAAF's Number 1 Transport and Movement Office (TMO) in Sydney and Number 5 TMO in Brisbane were able to provide adequate support for the fleet until the establishment of two RN Naval Aircraft Salvage Units (NASU) in Australia. These were NASU (S) based in Sydney and the smaller NASU (B) based in Brisbane. Their establishment, vehicles and personnel were only ever adequate to deal with average naval requirements but they continued to work under the direction of the relevant RAAF Transport and Movement Officer. This co-operation had the advantage that when the RN workload was high, the RAAF could lend its support but when it was low; the NASUs assisted the TMOs with RAAF commitments.

The number of ratings allotted to the original complement of MONAB 2 was inadequate for the designed output of 125 erected aircraft per month. As experience was gained, other units were added and the scheme of complement was constantly adjusted. With more experienced officers and senior ratings, some manpower savings could, undoubtedly, have been achieved but the continuing shortage of spares led to much nugatory work as we have already seen.

Because the war ended before it was expected to, the embarked squadrons were just able to cope with new aircraft from the Receipt and Despatch Units (RDUs) and those repaired by the FAMG. Attrition was high and very few aircraft reached the stage of becoming due for major inspections. Further, it was only during intermediate and main replenishment periods, when the fleet retired from the strike area, that aircraft other than flyable duds could be returned from the carriers. Thus only a few aircraft came back to the FAMG and rather less to the main base in Australia. It became apparent that the concept of providing a liberally equipped maintenance yard, the TAMY, was basically unsound because the aircraft that were returned mostly needed under 750 man/hours of repair work or minor inspections. The latter applied to aircraft that had been insufficiently maintained, something that came to be expected when the fleet carriers were operating under such intense pressure.

Moving aircraft all the way back to the main base in Australia for minor repairs made little sense and they

Aircraft engineering was manpower intensive in 1945. Ratings spread the starboard wing of a Seafire on **Implacable**'s *flight deck*

were better dealt with in the FAMG. It was well equipped to do the work and was much closer to the scene of operations. By July 1945 it was apparent that the strain under which the fleet carriers were working to achieve the flying task was making it increasingly difficult for the air engineers to carry out routine maintenance. Solutions to this problem were considered and the most likely to succeed was a plan to carry out routine maintenance in the replenishment carriers, keeping them close the operating areas for longer periods. This would have required a larger number of aircraft "in the pipeline" to the replenishment carriers and larger air engineering departments in the ships but had

the war continued beyond August; the scheme might well have improved matters.

In early 1945 squadron maintenance personnel moved ashore or embarked with their aircraft. This was not the most efficient use of manpower and the decision to form spare Carrier Air Groups (CAGs) led to a further decision, in principle, to adopt the USN system of Carrier Aircraft Servicing Units (CASUs) ashore and afloat. This would have necessitated the introduction of centralised maintenance with the majority of maintenance personnel remaining either ashore or afloat apart from a small team who moved with the aircraft. By August 1945 the complements of

several MONABs were being adjusted to make this feasible so that the new "streamlined" CAGs would find all the necessary support awaiting them for maintenance ashore and on board with no great interruption to the maintenance programme as they deployed.

THE LOGISTIC LIFELINE

The main problem to be solved by FONAP's Staff was the provision of aircraft ready for combat, trained aircrews and a considerable amount of air stores to the forward area some 4,000 miles from the main base in Australia. These had to be transferred to the fleet at sea during its temporary withdrawals from the operational area into designated service areas. These were as close to the combat area as was compatible with reasonable security from enemy interference.

The raw material to carry out this task consisted of:

• Aircraft which reached Australia from the UK, India, Ceylon and the USA. Some were erected and some crated. Those crated had to be erected and, together with those transported erect, these had to be extensively serviced to remedy damage, deficiencies or corrosion.

• Aircrew which reached Australia ostensibly fully trained. In practice, however, it was found that all needed refresher training, particularly in deck landing practice before joining a fleet carrier.

• Air stores which suffered from the fact that insufficient time had been allowed to build up reserves in Australia before the fleet arrived. As a result the requisite amounts of stores were

Fleet carriers of the BPF at anchor in Leyte Gulf, the Temporary Base, in April 1945.

seldom available when required. The problem was made even more difficult by the rate at which supplies finally arrived in Australia. This resulted in an accumulation beyond the capability of the available stores personnel and facilities to sort, stow and issue. Finally, new developments in operations and weapons produced new requirements from the fleet and these had usually to be met at first by improvisation or "borrowing".

The resources available to process the raw material were:

• The erection units MONAB 2, and later MONAB 7, and the TAMY which carried out erections, overhauls and modification programmes.
• The FAMG, later developed into the Air Train, which carried out similar duties afloat in the forward area.
• The other MONABs, which accommodated disembarked squadrons and carried out all training tasks.
• Maintenance Storage Reserve (MSR) Units, which, when attached to MONABs maintained reserve aircraft.
• The escort carriers (CVEs) which transported aircraft from one base to another and to the fleet at sea.

The core element of the plan was to establish the main base in Australia. This was to comprise the TAMY as the main repair organisation, an erection unit and a number of MONABs. The fleet was to return to Australia for refit and rehabilitation during the early stages of co-operation with the US Pacific Fleet. The next step was to be the creation of an intermediate base as far forward as possible in view of the great distance between the main base and the anticipated area of operations. This would need to have MONABs, but no TAMY, ashore and a suitable anchorage for the FAMG to which the fleet would return for major replenishment between successive operations. During operations, the service force including replenishment

carriers was to run a shuttle service to the service areas with a timetable arranged so that the fleet carriers would find the logistic support they needed when they withdrew between operations. The operations themselves were planned, typically on a five or six day cycle.

As the operational area advanced to the Japanese littoral it was anticipated that the intermediate base would be left too far behind and one or more forward bases would need to be established. These would incorporate airfields operated by MONABs as close as possible to sheltered anchorages. Unlike the main and intermediate bases, the forward base was to have the bare minimum of shore facilities and would serve principally as a floating store from which the service force would be replenished.

The BPF escort carrier force, the 30th Aircraft Carrier Squadron, was to be divided between ferry carriers and replenishment carriers. The former were to carry large loads of preserved aircraft to the intermediate base from the main base, the latter were to form part of the service force or fleet train. They were to carry a smaller number of combat-ready aircraft and replacement aircrew to the service areas from where they could be flown onto the fleet carriers at need. One of the escort carriers was to retain an embarked operational squadron for use as a CAP carrier to protect the service area, giving the fleet carrier air groups the chance of a rest.

As is often the case, even with the best-laid plans, things did not quite work out in the way originally intended by the planners in the UK. A party from *Unicorn* was disembarked in February 1945. This took a load of preserved aircraft to what was then RAAF Bankstown. With a great deal of assistance from the RAAF, this party prepared the aircraft for operational service in anticipation of the arrival of the fleet carriers. MONAB 1 arrived in Sydney on 18 December 1944 and, soon afterwards, took over the former RAAF base at Nowra. On 26 January 1945 MONAB 2, the first erection unit, lodged at Bankstown, which was then gradually taken over from the RAAF. On 27 January 1945 MONAB 3 arrived and was established at Schofields, despite the fact that it was far from complete.

Indeed, none of the shore establishments was anything complete when they were taken over but by the time the fleet arrived in Sydney in February 1945, FONAP was able to offer facilities for 100 disembarked aircraft and accommodation for 100 officers, 200 Chief and Petty Officers and 600 ratings. Sufficient replacement aircraft were prepared to replace the losses suffered by the fleet in Operation "Meridian" the attacks on the Sumatran oil refineries. During the period until the fleet sailed, every effort was made to build up reserves for Operation "Iceberg", the impending assault on Okinawa which was to be the BPF's first operation in the Pacific Theatre. When the fleet sailed on 27 February for Manus in the Admiralty Islands, a satisfactory position had been reached with reserves amounting to 20% of the embarked First Line Establishment (FAE) per month available. This was in accord with the losses suffered by the USN in recent operations.

Because there was no intermediate or forward base, however, all the escort carriers had to act at first as replenishment carriers carrying combat-ready aircraft from Australia to the service areas where they could be flown off to the fleet carriers. Fortunately, there was sufficient flexibility to accommodate this departure from the original plan because the ships were operational carriers rather than just ferry ships without flight decks. It meant, though, that they each had to be stored and equipped as completely as was possible to maintain all the types of aircraft in service with the BPF and to have the necessary complement of maintainers and general air ratings to maintain and operate them. In the event, their outfits fell well short of what was required but even this reduced the stock of available men and material available in Australia still further.

Five of the seven escort carriers that joined the BPF were fighter carriers with squadrons embarked. Two squadrons were disbanded and their pilots used to alleviate the critical shortage of replacements for the fleet carrier squadrons. The maintenance ratings remained in the ships to form the replenishment complement. Two other squadrons were taken out of their ships to form the basis of the spare carrier air group and the fifth, in *Speaker*, was retained to fly CAP sorties over the service area.

As plans were finalised for the BPF participation in Operation "Iceberg" it was decided to establish a temporary base with limited shore facilities in the Admiralty Islands. After protracted negotiations with the USN, permission was obtained to set up a MONAB on Ponam Island. MONAB 4 reached Sydney on 21 February 1945 and an advance party was sailed immediately to meet its equipment, which had proceeded directly to Ponam in SS *Clan Macauley*. It arrived on 11 March, the main party following a fortnight later. As will be seen in the chapter on MONAB 4, it proved extremely difficult to unload *Clan Macauley* since she had not been combat loaded and much of the equipment the MONAB needed was at the bottom of the hold, under other freight! In consequence, Ponam was of little value when the BPF arrived on 5 March but the FAMG was moored nearby and was able to provide support.

Reserve aircraft had been sent forward in *Unicorn*, *Striker* and *Slinger* and replacements required by the fleet after its passage north and a period of training off Manus were supplied by *Unicorn*. The transfer was found to be disconcertingly difficult, however because the lighters used by the British repair carrier proved difficult to operate in the heavy swell which was not unusual in the anchorage.

The BPF sailed from Manus for the US base at Ulithi on 17 March 1945. Prior to that the replenishment carriers *Striker* and *Slinger* together with the CAP carrier *Speaker* had gone on ahead to be ready in the service area. The decision was then taken, however, that the fleet would use Leyte Gulf in the Philippines as a forward anchorage for replenishment between the first two series of operations. In consequence the FAMG, with the remainder of the Fleet Train, moved there in late March. The BPF remained in the operational area, striking against Japanese airfields in the Sakashima Islands, for about four weeks. Throughout this time, replacement aircraft were provided by *Striker* and *Slinger*, which ran a shuttle between San Pedro Bay in Leyte Gulf and the service area, embarking fresh loads of aircraft from *Unicorn*. The fleet arrived in San Pedro Bay for an intermediate replenishment period on 23 April. While it was there,

Implacable refuelling from the RFA tanker *Olna* by the "abeam" method. The cruiser *Newfoundland* is on the other side of the tanker and *Victorious* is in the background.

Ruler replaced *Speaker* as CAP carrier.

The BPF sortied from Leyte Gulf for further strikes against targets in the Sakashima Islands and Formosa on 1 May 1945 and remained in the operational area until 25 May. By then, hits by Kamikaze aircraft had caused sufficient damage to warrant battle damage repairs in Australia. For that reason and the dwindling logistic support available from the Fleet Train, both BPF and Fleet Train sailed for Sydney, arriving on 5 June.

During these operations in support of Operation "Iceberg", a considerable amount of repair work was undertaken by the FAMG. Initially this comprised *Unicorn* alone but the component repair ship *Deer Sound* arrived at Manus on 9 April 1945 to support her. A problem manifested itself at this stage, howev-

er. Repaired aircraft needed to be test flown before being used as replacements but, whilst moored first at Manus and then at Leyte Gulf, *Unicorn* was unable to operate aircraft from her flight deck. Worse, after component or airframe changes, aircraft needed a compass swing and this had to be done away from large metal objects, such as a warship! There was thus a compelling need for an airfield to be available at the forward anchorage as there had been at Trincomalee during Eastern Fleet operations in 1944. This would have the additional advantages of being able to hold a larger pool of reserve aircraft than *Unicorn* and allowing reserve aircraft to be flown after their long haul from Australia to check their continued serviceability.

When the FAMG began to use San Pedro Bay in Leyte Gulf as the forward anchorage, a request was,

therefore, made to allow an MSR to be set up at the US Naval Air Station at Samar in the Philippines. Whilst the US authorities were warm to the idea, they could only accommodate 8 officers and 120 ratings by the end of May and 17 plus 240 by the end of June. Worse, Samar was 60 miles away from the anchorage in an isolated area poorly served by roads and it would be many weeks before sufficient RN transport could arrive. Captain Merewether of *Unicorn* recommended, therefore, that in the short term the forward aircraft pool should remain in *Unicorn* and this is what happened. She was replenished by *Fencer*, *Ruler* and Chaser on 11 and 27 April and 11 May 1945. When the majority of the BPF sailed for Australia at the end of May, *Unicorn* returned to Manus.

On 13 May 1945 the maintenance carrier *Pioneer* arrived in Sydney and added considerably to the FAMG's resources. It was re-organised as the Air Train under Commodore H.S. Murray-Smith RN, *Pioneer's* commanding officer who doubled as Commodore Air Train (COMAT). COMAT was responsible for carrying out FONAP's air logistic policy in the forward area but was immediately subordinate to Rear Admiral D.B. Fisher CB CBE, the Rear Admiral Fleet Train (RAFT). It was visualised that the ships of the Air Train might remain concentrated or be dispersed between two separate bases, as the situation demanded.

Meanwhile in Australia, the TAMY had arrived at Rocklea Camp near Brisbane on 27 March 1945. Two comfortable hostels were taken over for accommodation and work was initially split between Rocklea Factory where repairs were carried out and Archerfield where erection and overhaul took place. The TAMY

Implacable refuelling from RFA tanker *Wave Emperor* by the "astern" method. The destroyer *Ulysses* is on the tanker's starboard beam.

was originally designed to carry out only a limited number of erections but because production at Bankstown was below expectation, largely due to a shortage of spares, the TAMY had to fill the gap in order to meet the fleet's requirements. This was, at first, convenient because the lag in getting any damaged aircraft back to Australia was considerable. Since most aircraft were repaired by the FAMG, the number of aircraft arriving back at the TAMY never reached the proportions for which it had been designed.

In the original plan, only a limited number of airfields were expected to be established in Australia. These were for the use of air groups from carriers refitting, for training and the erection of aircraft newly arrived in the theatre. A greater number of airfields were expected to be set up at the intermediate base in the Philippines to repair damaged aircraft and accommodate air groups from replenishing carriers. Quite early in Operation "Iceberg" it became clear that there would be a considerable delay in establishing a permanent intermediate base in Leyte Gulf. In addition to Captain Merewether's concern about the remoteness of Samar from the anchorage, the USN needed all the facilities in the Philippines to support its Third and Seventh Fleets. On arrival in Australia, therefore, MONABs 5 and 6 were re-allocated, the former to Jervis Bay on 26 May and the latter to Maryborough on 30 May. It was intended that MONAB 5 should remain in Australia but MONAB 6 was to be kept ready to move forward when conditions allowed.

In June 1945, after careful consideration of operational needs, manpower and material available, the C-in-C decided against the construction of a full-scale intermediate base. It was estimated that it could have taken up to nine months to create, after the USN made space and facilities available and would be of little immediate value in supporting the BPF's next operations. He intended to use either Manus or a base in the Philippines on a more limited scale with minimal aviation facilities on shore. This decision had immediate ramifications in Australia, as more naval air stations would be required and negotiations were begun at once with the Australian authorities. After protracted discussion, it was agreed that MONAB 7 should be accommodated at Meeandah Camp near Brisbane and that Evans Head, Coffs Harbour and Narromine would be available for future MONABs with the possibility of two further airfields later.

During the two "Iceberg" periods of operation, there had never been a safe margin of reserve aircraft available. It was decided, therefore, to send two MSR units to RNAS Ponam in the Admiralty Islands in order to establish a subsidiary aircraft pool from which the forward pool at Samar could be more easily replenished. A Forward Aircraft Pool (FAP), consisting of an MM Unit, an MSR Unit and HQ Staff had been formed and equipped by early June and was embarked in *Pioneer* by 7 June. Before it sailed for Leyte Gulf, however, information was received that the next series of operations was to be against the mainland of Japan. The service areas would, therefore, be much further north than had been thought up till then. In consequence, it was decided that with the cycle of operations now proposed, the BPF could be supported from Manus, which was little further from the new service areas than Leyte Gulf and would save the haul between Manus and the Philippines. As a result, there was no longer a requirement for the FAP at Samar. However, since it was expected that some of the light fleet carriers might take part in the next operations and all four were to take part in Operation "Olympic", the invasion of Japan, an enlarged FAP was still essential. Permission was accordingly sought and obtained to establish the FAP as a lodger unit on the USN airfield at Pityilu in the Admiralty Islands. It sailed in *Pioneer* on 16 June and reached its destination on 21 June 1945.

The main body of the BPF left Sydney on 28 June and commenced operations against mainland Japan on 17 July. Four CVEs were employed as replenishment carriers because of the long haul from Manus to the service areas and were well able to meet the fleet's requirements. The FAP proved its worth and with the enlarged Air Train also at Manus, arrangements in the forward area were greatly improved compared with the earlier operations. Task Force 37 withdrew to Manus and later Australia on 12 August 1945, leaving *Indefatigable*, *King George V* and supporting consorts as Task Group 38.5 within the US Third Fleet

until VJ Day. They later entered Tokyo Bay for the formal surrender.

The war ended sooner than had been expected with the unconditional surrender of Japan after the atomic bomb attacks on Hiroshima and Nagasaki. By then, the BPF's logistic support organisation was in a period of transition having not yet built up to its full, planned extent. Thus, the fact that the Fleet Train was only able to support the BPF for a limited period in the forward area resulted in both the fleet and fleet train having to return, periodically, to the main base in Australia. With so many CVEs available to ferry aircraft from Australia, they could all have been given replenishment loads and sailed direct from the main base to the forward area. This would have minimised the requirement for the FAP at Manus. Equally, the fleet carriers were replenished with new aircraft when they returned to Australia and this eased the load on the FAP. However, the logistic plans were made for a long war and, had it continued as originally expected, the FAP would have proved its worth.

The Royal Navy's achievement in creating, almost from scratch, a logistic lifeline capable of supporting its deployed tactical air component many thousands of miles from the nearest friendly shore was a great one. The achievement of the whole fleet train allowed the BPF to remain at sea and in action for periods longer than any since the days of sail. The experience thus gained has underpinned the Royal Navy's ability to deploy and fight in the post 1945 world and its importance cannot be over-stated.

AIR STORES AND EQUIPMENT

The FONAP was responsible to the Commander-in-Chief BPF for the supply of aircrew, aircraft and engines to support the front line squadrons embarked in the fleet carriers. In practice and by force of circumstances, his staff had to do far more than this. They also had to act as advisers to the Directors of the Stores, Victualling and Air Stores organisations in Australia and to materially assist in the identification of stores and in processing the supply of urgent stores. Staff officers had to carry out a number of functions for which civilians in the Admiralty Stores Organisation would have been responsible in the UK. These included searching for local resources to manufacture items and forecasting the fleet's likely requirements during a replenishment period. There were no Supply Officers trained in air stores matters on the staffs of the C-in-C BPF, VA (Q) or ACS 1 and so the main work of attempting to meet user demand and attempting to address shortcomings fell on the staff of FONAP. This was a heavy commitment, which had not been allowed for when the size of the staff was projected in the UK. The following are some examples of the problems that had to be addressed:

- Local purchase and local repair orders

- Air transport services for vital stores
- Equipping replenishment and ferry carriers
- Organisation for the dispatch to, and return from, civilian contractors of airframes and engines
- Survey of unserviceable stores after return and arrangements for component repair
- Methods of dealing with repairable components sent back to the FAMG and ASIS by the BPF
- Organisation for the transfer and checking of aircraft from an RDU to a CVE, from a CVE to a FAP and from the pool to a front line squadron

When stores of all kinds arrived in Sydney, they were discharged at the docks and taken by road to the main store depot at Randwick, five miles from central Sydney. The storehouses were still under construction in early 1945 and permission had to be sought from the Allied Works Council to make use of sections as they neared completion. It was intended that Randwick would absorb all RAN stores activity in addition to the RN naval and air stores requirement. The office of the Superintending Naval Store Officer

Bombs on the flight deck of a fleet carrier during the replenishment period at Leyte Gulf

(SNSO) (Air) Sydney was located in the city centre. Thus the accounts and records were not at the depot. Demands from ships and air stations were sent to the office by post or delivered by transport in the most urgent cases. This was normal practice but it proved too slow to cope with the fast pace of activity in the BPF.

During their briefings at the Admiralty in November 1944, FONAP's staff officers were informed, before leaving for Australia, that stocks of aircraft stores and equipment would be available in Australia in large quantities early in the new year. It was also stated that a special outfit of equipment needed to erect aircraft had been despatched in the escort carrier *Atheling* to enable the first consignment of aircraft arriving in theatre to be erected. In December 1944, the amount of stores and equipment in Australia was negligible. Consequently, the plan that certain initial outfits were

to be supplied to MONABs and the FAMG by SNSO Sydney could not be complied with. As late as January 1945 the stores position was still unsatisfactory although large consignments were at least on their way. Arrangements were made with the RAAF for the RN to take over, as soon as possible, all stores and equipment useful to the Fleet Air Arm and surplus to RAAF requirements. Further arrangements were made for large-scale local manufacture of air stores wherever this proved possible.

The fleet carriers arrived in Sydney during the second week of February 1945 and sailed for the first operational period in the Pacific at the end of the month. They had been at sea for over three weeks on arrival at Sydney and had been instructed to lodge stock demands on SNSO Ceylon before sailing. They were told that any items not supplied in Ceylon would be forwarded later and were, thus, deemed to be stored

for six months when they arrived in Sydney and were not expected to make demands for stock replenishments until May. Demands on SNSO Sydney were to be limited to immediate and operational requirements. Despite this, demands far exceeded the range and quantity held by SNSO (Air) at Sydney at that time. A quantity of general spares was obtained from the RAAF and distributed and the arrival of the ASIS Fort Colville eight days before the fleet sailed made a difference. Despite all this, only 10% of the 2,300 demands made by fleet carriers had been met when the BPF sailed for Operation "Iceberg" and the extent to which operational demands had been impossible to meet gave cause for serious concern. Worse, many ships and air stations had outstanding demands that could not be met because the available stores had rightly been issued to the fleet carriers. The situation

was reviewed and reported to the Admiralty and, in consequence, a visit to the Admiralty by the Assistant Director of Stores (Pacific) (AD of S (P)) was arranged. Nothing could overcome the fundamental problem, however, which was the long delay between despatching stores in the UK and having them unpacked, identified and ready in Australia.

The BPF returned to Sydney early in June 1945 and conferences were held to discuss the best way of effecting improvements in the availability of air stores and equipment. Actions that appeared capable of improving matters included:

- Reducing the range and quantity of items carried in the fleet.
- An analysis of usage data to enable improved provisioning action to be taken.

*A pilot being returned to his carrier from the destroyer **Quadrant**.*

- The co-ordination of demands made by carriers in order to effect the best distribution of items in short supply.

As a result of these discussions, action was taken to instruct ships to land items held in excess of immediate requirements. AD of S (P) set up a team of experts that visited ships and analysed their expenditure. All the carriers were tasked to report their actual expenditure, as recorded in their store register records, over two given periods. It was further agreed that, in the absence of an air stores officer on the staff of ACS 1, the COMAT should co-ordinate requirements in the forward area. An air engineering specialist officer was provided for AD of S (P) to give advice in particular areas. These included:

- The likely consumption of spares that could be obtained from unserviceable items repaired in a carrier's own workshops.
- Operational items that had not been included in expenditure returns because they were unavailable and had not, thus, been issued.
- Likely flying intensity in BPF operations.
- The age and history of the various aircraft operating in different carriers.

The spares position was further helped by the arrival of the BPF's second ASIS, *Fort Langley*, in the forward area. She had arrived directly from Vancouver and was stored for all five aircraft types in 1 ACS. The

Admiralty also took steps to help the situation by appointing a Staff Supply Officer (Air) and a supporting team to the staff of COMAT. These comprised a Commander (S) RN, a Lieutenant Commander (S) RNVR, a Warrant Stores Officer and a number of specially trained stores and writer ratings. Working with them were to be an experienced civilian stores officer and three assistants. This organisation would probably have worked well and done much to improve matters still further but the war ended before it was in place.

The lack of air stores came closer than any other single factor to limiting the ability of the BPF to fight. The lack of time, before the formal creation of the BPF, to build up a quantity of stores in Australia was one factor as was the enormous distance between the UK and the BPF's main base. There were other, less obvious contributory factors though, including the time taken to construct and organise big store depots and the diluted, often inadequate, staffs available for handling air stores. By 1945 the RN was generally short of stores worldwide and conditions in the Pacific aggravated a greater problem. It is questionable whether the existing organisation for the procurement and distribution of air stores and material for the deployment of a carrier task force was adequate, even under the more favourable conditions in the UK. In his "Haul Down" report, FONAP recommended a post-war review of the Royal Navy's supply organisation, taking the BPF as the yardstick against which all future fleet operations should be judged.

THE PROVISION OF TRAINED AIRCREW

Replacement aircrew for the BPF came, in the main, from the Naval Operational Training Units (NOTU) in Ceylon. 706 Naval Air Squadron was formed in Australia to keep them in flying practice and to give refresher flying to aircrew who returned to active service from leave, hospital etc. In early 1945, there was an acute shortage of aircrew throughout the RN and none were available in Australia when the BPF arrived. When the flow from Ceylon started, it only provided a fraction of the number required and it

became necessary to disband some squadrons in order to make up the numbers in squadrons for the first Pacific operations and to provide a small reserve.

This shortage led, unfortunately, to some young aircrew being sent straight to the forward area in CVEs with no refresher flying. The long period without deck landing practice and, in some cases, without flying at all meant that some inexperienced pilots were unacceptable when they were required as replacements. To overcome this shortcoming, it was decided to form a

pool of reserve aircrew at Ponam. They were able to remain in flying practice by using the reserve aircraft and helped keep them serviceable. Further, it was decided to replace some of the Hellcats in the CAP carriers with Avengers and Corsairs so that replacement pilots could fly these aircraft on CAP and FRU sorties in the service areas in order to keep their deck landing skills up to scratch. By the end of the war, pilots were transferred from the replenishment carriers to the CAP carrier prior to joining fleet carrier squadrons. The system had not yet matured by VJ Day but was progressing well.

A large initial wastage of aircrew arose in the BPF because a number of pilots had either completed their front line tour or a substantial part of it on arrival in the Pacific Theatre. After "Iceberg" 1, it was realised that even a fresh pilot could not be expected to maintain fighting efficiency for 15 months in a first line squadron while engaged in such intensive operations as were conducted in the BPF. The ideal solution was the formation of spare Carrier Air Groups along USN lines but there were insufficient aircrew or aircraft for this at first. As an interim measure, a modified operational tour was introduced. In this, no pilot was to serve more than six consecutive months embarked. After six months, pilots were to serve four months ashore before returning to a carrier squadron. A limit of 18 months in an operational squadron was set; this was to begin when first embarked and was not to include periods working up ashore.

Sources:

- Report on the Organisation of the Flag Officer Naval Air Pacific in the Archive of the Fleet Air Arm Museum.
- Report of the Experience of the British Pacific Fleet - 1946 in the Archive of the Fleet Air Arm Museum.
- The Development of British Naval Aviation Volume III – unpublished document in the Author's collection.
- The Fleet Train by J D Brown. Published in the British Pacific & East Indies Fleet 50th Anniversary Document in 1995.
- The Forgotten Bases by J D Brown. Part of the Royal Australian Navy in World War II Second Edition edited by David Stevens. Published by Allen and Unwin, Crows Nest NSW, 2005

Chapter Two

THE AIR TRAIN

*Corsair fighter being hoisted from a lighter alongside **HMS Unicorn** by crane*

The Air Train, known at first as the Fleet Air Maintenance Group (FAMG), comprised a number of ships which provided mobile maintenance and repair facilities for carrier-borne aircraft in areas where shore-based support was either not available or too far distant. It comprised three types of ships known as aircraft maintenance ships, component repair ships and engine repair ships.

AIRCRAFT MAINTENANCE SHIPS

The need to provide maintenance facilities, in excess of those provided by *Unicorn*, was considered urgent from 1943 onwards. Options included the conversion of *Furious*, which was by then coming to the end of its operational life and the construction of specialist new ships. The former was rejected as too difficult and the latter course would have taken too long. The possibility of using escort carriers was rejected as it would have taken three to equate to the facilities provided by *Unicorn* and it was not the purpose for which the US Government had provided them under Lend/Lease arrangements. Ultimately it was decided that the need was important enough to justify the conversion of two of the early 1942 light fleet carriers already under construction in Vickers' yards into maintenance ships. *Edgar* and *Mars* were converted

and renamed *Perseus* and *Pioneer*. All flying equipment was removed and workshops were built onto the former flight deck. Since there was no need for sponsons, the light anti-aircraft armament was mounted on the upper deck.

These ships offered capabilities similar to those found in the Airframe Repair Shops (ARS) of a large naval air station or maintenance yard. They were able to carry out medium and minor repairs, mostly by replacement; major inspections of airframes and the implementation of modification programmes and medium scale repairs to fuselages. Workshops were also provided to carry out minor repairs and rectifications to aircraft engines, which could be run on test rigs prior to installation in aircraft. Functional tests of completed aircraft and their systems could be carried out on the former flight deck. Thus hydraulic systems, guns, radio and radar could be brought up to operational standard but compass swings and test flights could not be done. As they could not fly from these ships, aircraft had to be taken ashore by lighter and flight-tested from an airfield.

COMPONENT REPAIR SHIPS

The function of these ships was to keep the aircraft maintenance ships supplied with serviceable and tested components. In addition, they held themselves available to carry out emergency repair work, to support the fleet carriers and to produce components for the implementation of modification programmes. They were never utilised to their full extent by the BPF.

Their work was equivalent to that carried out by the various shops, other than ARS and Engine Repair Shops (ERS) at a naval air yard and comprised all repair work on components and accessories, particularly those known to be in short supply. Some idea of the extent of their capability can be gathered from their extensive workshop facilities. These included radar repair and test; metal workers and welding; coppersmiths; woodworking; fabric working; propeller; propeller balancing; dope and paint; oxygen and carbon dioxide bottle charging and test; machine shop; battery and accumulator repair; electrical repair; instrument repair; oleo and hydraulic; main plane, control surface and empannage shops.

ENGINE REPAIR SHIPS

These undertook work similar to that carried out in the ERS at a naval air yard. This included the complete overhaul, rectification and modification of aircraft engines and their accessories and their bench testing on completion of the work. They could not, however, work on power plant structures or carry out major salvage work. The ships stored and preserved a number of spare engines for use in the maintenance ships and for issue to fleet carriers.

A comprehensive outfit of spaces and workshops were built into these ships. These included engine receipt and unserviceable engine stores and shops for engine stripping, cleaning, and viewing. There were benches for engine accessory, carburettor and petrol testing and engine component rectification and assem- bly. There was extensive floor space for engine final assembly, electrical repair, engine test, test fan erection and stowage. Supporting facilities included woodworkers, metalworkers and machine shops together with provision for plating, battery charging, oxyacetylene and electric welding. There were storage and dispatch facilities for the various types of engine in use with the BPF.

The work process was not unlike a factory ashore but, built into a ship, was capable of movement to wherever the fleet support base needed to be. Engines were received direct from the carriers, from maintenance ships or from MONABs and taken into the receipt store. From there they were taken into the stripping shop where they were reduced to their com-

ponent parts. These were, in turn, taken to the cleaning bay for thorough cleaning before being taken to the viewing shop for visual and magnetic inspection. Next they would be dealt with in specialist shops such as the cylinder bay, valve-servicing bay and crankshaft bay. Parts that had been found unserviceable in the viewing process would be rectified or replaced with serviceable components. From there they would be taken to the component rectification and assembly bay and then built up in two final assembly lines that ran along either side of the ship, meeting in the electrical repair shop where the engine was completed with the fitting of the ignition system.

Once an engine had been assembled, it was taken to one of two test benches for trial runs before being put into a state of preservation, internally and externally.

Once preserved, it was taken to the engine despatch store to await issue to a maintenance ship or fleet carrier.

The three types of ship were intended to be complimentary but to avoid any delay in dealing with minor defects, small workshops of every sort were provided in the maintenance carriers. The Air Train accepted unserviceable aircraft and components from any source including the MONABs as well as the carrier force it was intended to support. To help this the different types of ship usually operated in close proximity as a group, tasking being centralised by a Group Staff Office in one of the ships. HMS *Unicorn*, the repair carrier, was unique in that she combined all these functions within one hull that was also capable of launching and recovering aircraft.

THE MAINTENANCE PROCESS

In appearance, the two maintenance carriers looked very like their half sisters, the light fleet carriers. The upper deck was still known as the "flight deck" despite being unable to operate fixed wing aircraft. The two lifts were retained to move aircraft between this deck and the hangar below. The island, enlarged across the deck by a big box-like structure, contained air offices, a ground equipment store and recreational facilities including a cinema. At the after end of the upper deck was a rectangular building, which contained the oxygen production plant and stowage for spare engines.

Surrounding the hangar and running the full length of the ship were two decks, the upper known as the gallery deck, the lower as the hangar deck. Each of these was divided into various compartments. For instance the gallery deck housed the radar and electrical offices and repair shops; the ready use stores; the instrument repair shop; the spark-plug servicing shop; woodworkers' shop; dope store; blacksmiths' and welders' shops. The hangar deck contained the ground equipment and tool stores; the fabric workers' shop; hydraulic and oleo leg shop; dope shop; ERS and fuel pump shop; armament offices; metal workers' shop; machine shop; propeller shop and parachute hanging

room. The decks below the flight deck contained accommodation spaces and machinery compartments.

Unserviceable aircraft were brought to the ship by two aircraft lighters. These were lifted on board by crane and stowed in cradles on the upper deck when the ship was at sea. Each lighter had a flat deck 48 feet long by 12 feet wide with lashing points to secure aircraft in transit. They were both powered by two V8 petrol engines of 40 horsepower. The ship also carried two 23 knot "skimmers" each powered by a 45 horsepower diesel, two fast motor boats, a motor cutter and a pinnace. There were also several mobile cranes or "Jumbos" to move crated stores, components and equipment to any part of the upper deck or hangar.

As soon as an aircraft arrived on board, it was taken on charge by the Receipt and Despatch Section. Guns were made safe and any bombs or pyrotechnics removed to safe stowage. All "Appendix A" items such as instruments, radio, safety equipment and armament were then removed and the aircraft's log books thoroughly checked. At this stage the aircraft was still on the upper deck and it would undergo a preliminary inspection to see whether or not it was worth repairing. As a rough 'rule of thumb', an aircraft that

needed more than 1,000 man-hours would not be repaired. Should it be deemed worthy of repair, a Board of Survey would follow. This would provide a complete assessment of damage and functionally test the electrical and hydraulic systems. If fit, an engine run would be carried out to assess its serviceability. If an airframe was deemed unsuitable for repair within the Air Train, a decision would have to be taken whether to arrange for its return to the TAMY in Australia in a suitable ferry carrier or simply to push it over the side having stripped the airframe of everything useful.

Next, the aircraft would have been taken down into the hangar where the ARS would take it on charge. Those components allocated to the component repair ship would be removed and shipped across; others, requiring minor amounts of work, could be repaired on board. The main hangar was a large space, including the dope and propeller shops.

As the aircraft was worked on, it moved progressively along the hangar until it reached the re-assembly stages. While the airframe was worked on, its various components made their way through workshops. Electrical equipment was stripped, cleaned and, if necessary, replaced. Batteries were charged in a room in which two motor generators, driven from the ship's ring main, supplied current at up to 40 volts DC. Instruments, such as the airspeed indicator, would have been removed and re-calibrated. Radios and wireless sets were re-calibrated in test rooms equipped with artificial aerials. Hydraulic equipment such as oleos were tested on static rigs and replaced if they were found unserviceable. Damaged airframes were repaired using the resources of the metal repair shops.

These were equipped with wheeling and raising machines, guillotines, bending machines and rolls, metal nibblers, bench drills and all the necessary workbenches. Fabric repairs were carried out in extensive fabric repair shops equipped with sewing machines and large work tops.

Once reassembled, the aircraft was taken to the upper deck and test run. Guns could be fired and radios checked. The aircraft would then be near an operational condition but would have to be taken ashore for a compass swing and check test flight. It was then fit to be taken into the supply chain for the operational fleet.

This was a very sophisticated system but it was biased heavily toward repair, based on the experience gained by the Royal Navy in the first five years of war. The US Navy, with its larger production base, relied more heavily on replacement than repair. It had no equivalent to the maintenance ships and relied on large numbers of ferry carriers that stocked supply pools in the forward area. Interestingly though, the US Army Air Force commissioned aircraft maintenance ships to support the B 29 squadrons that operated from remote islands in the Pacific. These were closely comparable to the Royal Navy's Air Train but were manned with merchant navy sailors and USAAF maintenance personnel. In addition to lighters, larger versions of the sort used by the British, they carrier Sikorsky R4 helicopters to ferry passengers and light stores. They were the first ships to operate helicopters on a regular basis.

Office of the Commander-in-Chief
British Pacific Fleet

BPF/1043P   13 June 1945

MEMORANDUM

DIRECTIVE FOR THE COMMODORE AIR TRAIN
(Short title COMAT)

1. Commodore Air Train is responsible to the Rear Admiral Fleet Train for the air logistic support of the Fleet in the forward area, including:-

    a. Supplies
        i.   of aircraft
        ii.   of aircrews and maintenance personnel
        iii. of air stores

2. Maintenance and repair of aircraft in the forward area, both FAMGs and ashore, in conformity with the policy of FONAP.

3. The Air Train will form a sub-command of the Fleet Train and will consist of the following categories:-

    a. Aircraft Repair Ships.
    b. Aircraft Maintenance Ships.
    c. Aircraft Component Repair Ships.
    d. Aircraft Engine Repair Ships.
    e. CVEs (for operation but not for administration).
    f. Air Store Issue Ships.

4. Operational control of the Air Train:

    a. CVEs
        To be operated by RAFT in the forward area, as advised by COMAT, in accordance with the logistic plan for any operation.

    b. Aircraft Repair Ships and Air Store Issue Ships
        Disposition of these forces will be generally controlled by RAFT to meet Fleet requirements, in accordance with the policy of FONAP.

5. Administration of the Air Train:

    a. CVEs to be administered by the Type Commander (Commodore Commanding 30th Aircraft Carrier Squadron), who will be responsible to the Commander-in-Chief BPF.

b   Aircraft repair Ships and Air Store Issue Ships to be administered by COMAT who will be responsible to RAFT except in relation to technical air questions regarding which he will deal direct with FONAP.

c.   Reserve Aircrews and Forward Air Drafting Pool to be administered by COMAT, communicating direct with Commodore RN Barracks Sydney and FONAP.

6.   COMAT is authorised to deal direct with:-

a.   FONAP on technical matters.

b.   MONABs in the forward area with regard to the provision of reserve aircraft and crews and aircraft reserve.

7.   Logistic Planning

Commodore Air Train is responsible to Flag Officers Commanding Aircraft Carrier Squadrons for detailed logistic planning for each specific operation. These plans are to be framed in accordance with FONAP policy. After they have been concurred in by RAFT, who will co-ordinate them with the general logistic plan, they will be issued in COMAT's own name and executed by him.

                                            (signed)
                                            Bruce Fraser
                                            Admiral

COMMODORE AIR TRAIN

Report on the experience gained during the Air Logistic Support of the British Pacific Fleet

March to August 1945

Part One

1.　　Operations against the Ryukyu Islands during March, April and May 1945.

　　a.　　The carrier force consisted of HM Ships *Indomitable*, *Indefatigable*, *Victorious*, *Illustrious*, *Speaker* and *Formidable*, the last named replacing *Illustrious* half way through the operation. The total embarked strength in these ships was 246 aircraft.

　　b.　　Before the operation started, the force was brought up to strength by embarking 29 aircraft from RNAS Ponam in the Admiralty Islands. Thereafter the force was supplied from Leyte in the Philippines.

　　c.　　Air logistic support was provided by HM Ships *Unicorn*, *Deer Sound* and *Fort Colville*, which lay in Leyte Gulf with the main body of the Fleet Train.

　　d.　　During these operations, all replacement aircraft were shipped from Australia in escort carriers to RNAS Ponam (2,300 miles) and Leyte (1,500 miles further) and, apart from 44 supplied direct to the carriers at Leyte at the end of April, were then taken in replenishment carriers 700 miles from Leyte to the replenishment area.

　　e.　　No airfield was available at Leyte for servicing reserve aircraft or for establishment of a reserve pool. HMS *Unicorn* and any escort carriers which were, from time to time, available had to undertake this work.

　　f.　　The following replacement aircraft were transferred to the carrier force during the March – May operation:

　　　　　　29 from RNAS Ponam to bring the force up to strength
　　　　　　56 by replenishment CVEs in three replenishments
　　　　　　44 at Leyte
　　　　　　117 by replenishment CVEs in five replenishments
　　　　　　In addition 40 aircraft were sent forward in replenishment CVEs but were not required by the fleet and 29 unserviceable aircraft were returned by the fleet in replenishment CVEs.

　　g.　　Choice of types of aircraft to be sent forward in replenishment carriers was based on forecasts of likely wastage. During the first month of operations, the principal needs were for more Seafire, Firefly and Hellcat. The second month produced an unexpected call for Avenger and Corsair, but lack of an adequate reserve pool prevented the loading of replenishment carriers

from being varied sufficiently to meet the demands of the fleet. This inflexibility caused the shipment forward of many of the 40 unwanted aircraft mentioned in paragraph 6.

h.   All aircraft transfers at Leyte were carried out by *Unicorn's* two B type lighters. They were only just adequate for the work, having to run 24 hours a day for a week during the replenishment period at the end of April. In a sheltered harbour, these lighters are excellent, but they are lively in a swell, and one aircraft was lost overboard.

i.   The long haul from Australia to Leyte proved detrimental to the aircraft in the ferry carriers, and most of these aircraft had to be transferred to *Unicorn* at Leyte for servicing, rectification of minor defects and incorporation of operational modifications before they were fit for transfer to the fleet. Shortage of personnel in the ferry carriers, both in numbers and experience, and lack of a scheme for protecting them from corrosion, contributed to this state of affairs and lack of an airfield at Leyte, at which to do the work, threw a heavy burden on *Unicorn*.

j.   During this period of operation, the number of aircraft held for repair in *Unicorn* varied from 19 to 11, at an average of 16. The number held for servicing and modification varied from 38 to 8 at an average of 17. Altogether, 105 aircraft passed through *Unicorn's* workshops for repair, modification and/or servicing before delivery to the fleet.

Lessons Learnt

Provision of an airstrip at the forward base is essential, so that aircraft ferried from the main base can be landed, serviced, modified if necessary and flown before embarkation in replenishment carriers.
Provision of a pool of reserve aircraft at the forward base is essential, so that the loading of replenishment carriers can quickly be varied to suit the changing requirements of the fleet.
The complements of replenishment carriers must be adequate to keep the embarked aircraft in full operational serviceability. The replenishment load with its flight deck cargo forbade flying tests.
Aircraft shipped in ferry carriers from the main base must be modified as near to operational standard as possible and must be preserved to a degree sufficient to prevent corrosion and petty unserviceability arising on passage.

Part Two

1.   Operations against the Japanese Mainland during July and August 1945.

a.   The major replenishment period of the fleet at Sydney gave time to profit to some extent from the earlier lessons. For the new series of operations:

b.   Replenishment was carried out from the Admiralty Islands, where airstrips were available at Ponam, manned by MONAB 4, and Pityilu, manned by the newly formed RN Forward Aircraft Pool.

c.   A small pool of reserve aircraft was built up at Ponam and Pityilu before the fleet's arrival. It totalled 107 aircraft, of which 41 were operationally ready and a further 35 were expected to be ready within a fortnight.

d.   The complements of replenishment carriers were increased from the drafting pool at Sydney, and the Forward Area Specialist Maintenance Party was formed. This latter consisted of about twelve experienced ratings drawn from the operational carriers and led by three officers. They were placed at the disposal of the Commodore Air Train and were allocated, by him, to the replenishment carriers.

e.   Most of the aircraft shipped from Sydney to the Admiralty Islands were put in a state of Class II preservation which improved their condition on receipt though it was not complete proof against corrosion.

f.   HMS *Pioneer*, flying the broad pennant of the Commodore Air Train arrived at the Admiralty Islands on 21 June 1945 and established the RN Forward Aircraft Pool at Pityilu. She was joined by HMS *Deer Sound* on 24 June and by HMS *Unicorn* on 21 July. RFA *Fort Langley* arrived at Manus during July direct from Vancouver and *Fort Colville* rejoined shortly before the armistice. The carrier force consisting of HM Ships *Implacable*, *Indefatigable*, *Victorious*, *Formidable* and *Ruler* had a total embarked force of 274 aircraft.

g.   During these operations, replacement aircraft were shipped from Australia to the Admiralty Islands, a distance of 2,300 miles in escort carriers and, once, in *Unicorn*. Most of these air craft were in a state of Class II preservation and were landed at Pityilu for servicing. Replenishment loads were embarked in replenishment carriers by lighter from Pityilu and taken forward 2,500 miles to the replenishment area.

h.   The following replacement aircraft were transferred to the fleet or replenishment carriers dur ing the July – August operations:

> 28 at Manus to bring the force up to strength.
> 155 to replenishment carriers in 7 replenishment loads.

Of these replacements, the last load of 17 returned as they did not reach the fleet before VJ Day and 18 out of the previous loads were not required. 52 unserviceable aircraft were brought back to Manus by replenishment carriers. These were surveyed by Commodore Air Train's staff and allocated:

> to *Pioneer* or *Unicorn* up to their capacity, or
> to the FAP for preservation and ultimate return to Australia for repair.

i.   For these transfers, *Pioneer*'s two 'B' type lighters were available and, after *Unicorn*'s arrival, her two lighters came into service. An extra lighter which had been embarked by *Pioneer* in Sydney needed a lot of refitting and did not come into service until about the end of July.

j.   Due to the three mile haul from Pitylu to the fleet anchorage, this lighter capacity was insuffi cient. Several times it was necessary to borrow an American 'NL' Pontoon which could carry three or four aircraft at a time, and was yet able to go alongside the pier at Pityilu with its four to five foot draft.

k.   While at Manus, *Pioneer* repaired 24 aircraft in 8 weeks and, after test flight, transferred them to the RN FAP. *Unicorn* repaired 8 aircraft in the five weeks she was present, in addition to preparing 18 aircraft for service from Class II preservation.

l.   The RN FAP, which was established by *Pioneer* at Pityilu by 11 July, was responsible for main taining the reserve aircraft at readiness to embark in replenishment carriers. It also undertook the de-preserving of aircraft shipped from Australia and received and preserved those of the damaged aircraft brought back from the fleet which were allocated by COMAT for ultimate return to Australia.

m.   The FAP lodged with the Americans and its equipment included two Dorland hangars, one ten-ton mobile crane and a small quantity of motor transport and ground equipment collected from Australia.

n.   During the July/August operations, the FAP handled the landing or embarkation of 348 air craft, only one being damaged in the process.

o.   The most onerous work of the FAP was to keep the reserve aircraft serviceable in the climate at Pityilu, which included heavy downpours of rain almost daily. The general humidity made most aircraft unserviceable every morning. It was found necessary to fly reserve aircraft every five days and take them up to 10,000 feet to dry them out properly, and this in itself caused considerable work.

Pioneer and *Unicorn* each disembarked a small test flight party to lodge with the RN FAP, these parties being responsible for bringing the aircraft repaired in their ships up to full opera tional readiness before transferring them to the Pool. Compass swinging was the only service not so dealt with, as neither ship carried an observer.

Sources:

• Report on the Organisation of the Flag Officer Naval Air Pacific in the Archive of the Fleet Air Arm Museum.
• Report of the Experience of the British Pacific Fleet - 1946 in the Archive of the Fleet Air Arm Museum.

Chapter Three

HMS UNICORN

HMS Unicorn *in Seapa Flow.*

DESIGN BACKGROUND

Although she looked like a small operational aircraft carrier, *Unicorn* was a rather more unusual ship. She was the first aircraft carrier in the world to be built for a specific, narrowly defined purpose rather than for general aviation duties. Throughout her short but eventful career she had the tallest bridge in the Royal Navy at 95 feet and the highest mast at 167 feet. She was the first ship in any navy capable of carrying out the full range of aircraft maintenance and repair work in addition to the ability to operate aircraft from the flight deck.

Her origins lay in the Abyssinian Crisis of 1935/36 when the Royal Navy learnt about the logistical sup-port needed to maintain a deployed carrier strike fleet at some distance from the UK. From the reinforced Mediterranean Fleet's operations it was calculated that a carrier could lose up to 20% of its air group in action or damaged beyond repair in 'operational crashes'. A further 10% could be grounded by the need for major repair that could not be carried out in a fleet carrier. Although based on theory because the Crisis did not lead to conflict, the numbers proved to be remarkably accurate in subsequent operations in the Pacific. The figures were bad enough when applied to the pre-war carriers such as *Glorious* and *Ark Royal* with air groups of 48 and 60 respectively, but the armoured carriers of the Illustrious class were only to be capable of operating 36. If one third of these were damaged beyond repair, support and replacement on a large scale was clearly necessary. The man who conceived the armoured carriers was also responsible for the solution to this problem.

Admiral Sir Reginald Henderson GCB was an imaginative officer who had specialised in Gunnery and served in the battleship *Erin* at Jutland. He served in the Admiralty as Director of the anti-submarine division from late 1916 and did much to prove that convoys were the best means of protecting merchant shipping. In 1926 he took command of the aircraft carrier *Furious* and, after promotion to Rear Admiral, became the first Rear Admiral Aircraft Carriers (RAAC). With three carriers under his command he developed carrier strike tactics that were ahead of those in use in the USA and Japan despite the negative

influence of the RAF which wanted to concentrate national resources on the production of land-based bombers. He was a staunch advocate of dive bombing, again having to fight RAF opposition. In 1934 he became Controller, the Admiralty Board member responsible for new warship and weapons projects. He worked directly with W A D Forbes, the ADNC Carriers, to force through the armoured carriers, as he wanted ships that could stand up to attack by land-based bombers. He was insistent that the maintenance and repair carrier that became *Unicorn* should support them in the same way that submarine and destroyer depot ships supported their flotillas. He was also far-sighted enough to insist that the ship should have all the essential features of an operational carrier, thus giving the fleet an extra deck in time of need. Admiral Henderson was forced by ill health to resign in March 1939 and he died only two months later.

Unicorn shortly after completion.

Unicorn with Force V during the Salerno landings with a Seafire in the recovery pattern.

She was a very complicated design and preparatory work took over a year before her keel was laid down at Harland & Wolff's Belfast Yard on 29 June 1939. The final approved design was intended to provide comprehensive support to a carrier task force and her two hangars were intended both to store reserve aircraft and carry out extensive repair and maintenance work. It was expected that up to 48 aircraft could be embarked and space was available in the hangars for some of them to spread and fold their wings whilst struck down. In addition to the large engine repair workshop, she had a test compartment in which engines could be run at full power after repair work. The support was expected to go beyond maintenance work, however, and she had a large Sick Bay, an Operating Theatre and a Dental Surgery. Space for two emergency medical stations was also provided to cope with action casualties. Her armament of four twin 4-inch mountings and pom-poms was in line with

contemporary depot ship practice.

Unicorn was fitted with an elaborate system of hoists and transfer rails in her two hangars to facilitate component repair in aircraft undergoing repair and the after end of the upper hangar was open to allow aircraft engine runs without the aircraft having to be taken to the flight deck. The flight deck extended a long way aft over the opening so that a self-propelled aircraft lighter could be suspended beneath it. This could be lowered flush with the upper hangar deck so that aircraft could be moved onto it and conveyed, once the lighter was lowered into the water, to another carrier or shore base. Alternatively, aircraft could be lowered onto the lighter, once it was afloat, by crane. She was fitted out with an extremely comprehensive range of airframe, engine, radio and electrical workshops and was designed to have a stores complex capable of carrying spare parts for the entire contemporary range of front line aircraft in service with the

Fleet Air Arm. By the time she completed in 1943, however, it would no longer have been big enough to cope with the increased number of types in service; especially those built in the USA. Despite some criticism that she was over-complicated, she was a most successful support ship without which naval air operations in the East Indies, Pacific and Korea war zones would not have been practical.

In view of the desperate need for operational carriers, the decision was taken in 1942 to hasten her completion without the complete outfit of workshop equipment for use with the Home and Mediterranean Fleets. She was launched on 20 November 1941 and completed with the reduced capability on 12 March 1943.

AN OPERATIONAL CARRIER

On completion she was allocated to the Home Fleet and after commissioning, she worked up in the Firth of Clyde. During this period this ship was reckoned to be part of the "BEF Flotilla", the initials standing for

"Back Each Friday". Her ship's company became familiar with Ailsa Craig and the anchorage off Lamlash. Her first operational sortie was in May 1943 with an air group comprising 887 Naval Air Squadron

*A damaged Seafire being unloaded from **Unicorn** after the Salerno operation. LR 706 had served with 879 squadron in **Attacker** and had been badly damaged on 10 September 1943 when flown by Sub Lieutenant R J H Grose. It shows the three types of damage that were common in the early Seafires - broken propeller tips from the aircraft "pecking" nose down on landing, a broken back from a heavy landing and structural damage aft.*

Unicorn's batsman on the port side aft. Note the relatively small island with the Type 72 homing beacon on the mast and the port anti-aircraft barrage director over the compass platform.

equipped with Seafires together with 818 and 824 Naval Air Squadrons with Swordfish. She fulfilled the dual purposes of escorting Convoy MKF 15 to Gibraltar and ferrying RAF Beaufighter aircraft to the Rock. Whilst operating with the convoy, *Unicorn* was attacked by a Focke Wulf Condor, bombs from which fell near the starboard side. No damage was done to *Unicorn* or any ship in the convoy. The return journey was uneventful except for a single attack at dusk in very poor visibility by a single enemy aircraft that was not seen. Its bombs fell wide of the convoy.

On return to home waters, a further period of operational training was carried out in the Clyde areas before joining the Home Fleet at Scapa Flow. In July 1943, *Unicorn* sailed in company with *Illustrious* for Operation "Governor", a feint against the South

Norwegian coast intended to divert German attention from the assault on Sicily. The air group remained as it had been for the Gibraltar run. The material effects of this operation were minimal but it showed that a carrier task force could operate with impunity within 150 miles of the enemy held Norwegian coast in spite of being sighted by enemy reconnaissance aircraft. Indeed, five Blohm and Voss Type 138 flying boats were shot down by Martlets from *Illustrious*. After returning with the Home Fleet, *Unicorn* returned to the Clyde in order to embark two new Seafire squadrons, 809 and 897 to add to 887. The Swordfish squadrons disembarked, with the exception of a detachment of 818 for anti-submarine protection. In August, *Unicorn* deployed to Gibraltar where she joined the escort carriers *Attacker*, *Battler*, *Hunter* and **Stalker** to form Force V under Rear Admiral Sir Phillip Vian. The Force was to give fighter cover to Operation "Avalanche", the allied landings at Salerno, with 110 Seafires embarked in the five carriers. The carriers gave allied planners the flexibility to land where they chose, unencumbered by the limited radius of action of land-based fighters. Heavy cover, against the possibility of intervention by the Italian Fleet, was provided by Force H comprising **Illustrious** and **Formidable** supported by the battleships **Warspite**, **Valiant**, **Nelson** and **Rodney**.

The Force moved to the operational area via Algiers and an intensive work up off Malta. **Unicorn** was passing through the Straits of Messina when news of the Italian surrender was received but the assault began as planned on 9 September 1943. **Unicorn** flew 75 sorties on the first day, the fighters being used to provide a Combat Air Patrol (CAP) over the landings throughout the daylight hours and to patrol the sea

approaches out to 40 miles. During the three and a half days of the assault phase **Unicorn's** Seafires flew 198 sorties and fighters from the force were involved in seven air combats and shot down two enemy aircraft. The low wind made it difficult for the inexperienced pilots to land on the escort carriers with their 18 knot top speed and attrition was high. With her higher speed and larger deck, **Unicorn** was better placed but damage took its toll and the number of sorties reduced as the operation progressed. 60 were flown on 10 September, 44 on the next day and only 18 on 12 September. By then a forward airstrip had been established ashore at Paestum and two Seafires were disembarked to it.

Great credit was due to the squadrons and the flight deck handling parties because the early Seafires did not have folding wings and were difficult to manoeuvre on deck and to strike down into the hangar. The ship's small aircraft repair section worked hard to

Unicorn shortly after arriving in Trincomalee in February 1944. **Renown** and **Illustrious** are visible in the background.

The Blacksmiths' workshop.

repair damaged aircraft and managed to produce ten aircraft over-night after the third day's operations. Aircraft from Seafire and Martlet squadrons in the carriers of Force H were also embarked to help make up the numbers. As more land-based fighters were able to fly into the beach-head, Force V withdrew to Bizerta where it stood by in case it was needed to return to support the troops ashore against a German counter-attack. In the event, Force V was not needed

and *Unicorn* returned to the UK on 20 September. She took with her damaged Seafires from the Mediterranean Theatre and, once she had disembarked her own squadrons, they were landed at the King George V Dock in Glasgow from where they were transported to RN Air Yards for repair. In October she returned to Harland & Wolff's shipyard for a refit and completion in her designed role as an aircraft repair ship.

THE FIRST AIRCRAFT REPAIR SHIP

While *Unicorn* was deployed as an operational carrier, a carefully selected team of officers and men were sent to air yards in the Home Air Command to train for their tasks in the first aircraft repair ship in any navy. They joined their new ship during December 1943 and sailed with her on 29 December for service in the expanding Eastern Fleet commanded by Admiral Somerville. She sailed in company with *Illustrious* which flew the flag of Rear Admiral Moody, Rear

Admiral (Air) Eastern Fleet. They joined Vice Admiral Power, the new Second-in-Command of the Eastern Fleet off the Hebrides, flying his flag in *Renown* with the other ships of the First Battle Squadron, *Queen Elizabeth* and *Valiant* in company. The size and quality of these reinforcements showed that the balance of the Royal Navy's heavy units was shifting to the Far East.

The enemy did not challenge the force as it made its

way past Gibraltar at night and then along the North African coast. *Unicorn* led the other warships through the Suez Canal on 12 January 1944 with a brief stop at Aden for fuel on 19 January. After Aden she parted company and headed for RNAS Cochin in Southern India where she delivered a consignment of aircraft for the Receipt and Despatch Unit (RDU) on 27 January. Whilst at sea, her engineers prepared crated Barracudas for operational service and she operated anti-submarine patrols with 818, her long-standing Swordfish squadron. In addition to those tasks, she provided a spare deck so that Corsair and Barracuda pilots from Illustrious could practice their deck landing skills away from the cramped deck of the fleet carrier. Admiral Moody praised her obvious success in these different roles.

On 2 February 1944, *Unicorn* arrived at Trincomalee, which was to be her base port for several months. Once there, she acted in her designed role as a mobile air base in support of the 1st Aircraft Carrier Squadron, which grew to comprise *Victorious* and *Indomitable* as well as *Illustrious*. In addition to aircraft, engine and component repair work whilst moored in the harbour, she sailed frequently to give deck landing training for the growing number of pilots passing through the Naval Operational Training Units (NOTU) in Ceylon. She proved her worth as the only functioning repair organisation close to the fleet capable of supporting the fleet carriers and their squadrons. Admiral Moody said, in his Reports of Proceeding, that without her the Eastern Fleet's strike and fighter squadrons could not have remained operational.

In addition to her routine tasks, *Unicorn* was sent, occasionally, to Colombo to re-stock with stores, the first such visit being made on 21 March 1944. In May she carried out a docking and essential defect repair

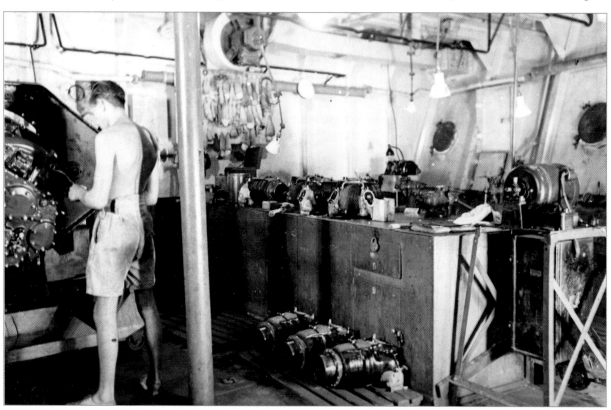

A corner of the radial engine workshop in 1945.

The propeller workshop.

period in Bombay before returning to "Repair Alley" in Trincomalee where she moored with other depot and support ships. Barracudas and Corsairs were repaired in her hangars using a rolling "production line" technique that worked well and was to prove a sound basis for the later, higher-pressure work in the Pacific. She maintained her own test flight party ashore at RNAS China Bay where aircraft that had completed their repairs were taken. Once there they were flown by the ship's maintenance test pilots and their compasses were swung. When signed off as serviceable they were allocated to the reserve aircraft pools at air stations ashore.

In August, 818 Swordfish squadron which had been with *Unicorn* from her original commissioning was at first lent to *Atheling* and then disbanded, its aircrew being converted onto the Avenger TBR aircraft and the maintainers going into the Eastern Fleet drafting pool. Since she was not a fleet carrier, *Unicorn* did not have

a Royal Marines Band. However, during her stay in Trincomalee, her ship's company produced a Fife and Drum Band which worked very well and provided music both for Sunday Divisions on the flight deck and church, afterwards, on the quarter-deck. Like many other British warships, she was not insulated or air-conditioned for tropical service and the heat below decks led to many cases of Prickly Heat.

American aircraft were joining the fleet in ever-increasing numbers. These differed in many ways from those built in Britain, not least in having different threads on the nuts and bolts and different electrical systems. Even washers and wiring looms differed and a completely new range of general and specific stores items had to be stocked on board. Ratings intended to work on US built aircraft had to undergo special training, in the USA for some of the senior ratings, and were issued with different, US-specific, tool kits. For convenience a number of these where

Propeller stowage rack in the lower hangar. Note the preserved Corsair in BPF markings. Doped fabric was used to cover areas, such as the wing-fold, where salt laden moisture could get into the airframe and cause corrosion.

The radial power plant stowage in the lower hangar, 1945.

Reserve Corsair and Firefly aircraft, in their preservative coatings, stored in the lower hangar.

Part of the 'in-line' engine workshop in 1945.

formed into Special Repair Parties (SRP) to carry out specific repair and modification work on American supplied Lend/Lease aircraft. These were to be the genesis of the concept of Mobile Storage and Repair (MSR) Units that formed an important part of the MONAB organisation a year later. Several SRPs were drafted to *Unicorn* during 1944 to support modification work on the Fleet's American supplied aircraft. They found that the ship was not laid out for concurrent work on the two different varieties of aircraft and engine. Ideally she needed two production lines and different shops for British and US aero-engines. These would require structural alterations and the fitting of extra engineering equipment in both hangars and workshops. With the decision to go ahead with the formation of a British Pacific Fleet, *Unicorn* was ordered to proceed to Durban where this work could be put in hand as quickly as possible.

Unicorn left Trincomalee in early November with the Barracudas of 817 squadron embarked for anti-submarine protection. She made refuelling stops at Addu Atoll in the Maldive Islands on 8 November and Diego Suarez in Madagascar on 13 November before passing through the Mozambique Channel to South Africa. She crossed the Equator for the first time on 9 November and arrived in Durban on 19 November 1944, where Miss Perla Siedle Gibson, the "White Lady", gave her the famous singing welcome. Ten days leave was given to the ship's company while the work was carried out and most accepted invitations to visit private homes organised by the South African Women's Auxiliary Services and the Navy War Fund.

Modified to be able to repair and support the five different types of aircraft intended for use in the BPF, American built Corsairs, Hellcats, Avengers and British built Fireflies and Seafires, *Unicorn* left Durban on 1 January 1945, re-crossing the Equator on 11 January. Her first destination was Colombo, off which she carried out a period of deck landing training to qualify pilots for operational service with the BPF. Her next task was to ferry reserve aircraft and engines to Australia from both Cochin and Colombo. *Unicorn* emptied the Eastern Fleet's air stations of their reserve stock and embarked a record 82 aircraft and 120 aero-engines for transit to Sydney. She could have taken more had they been available.

Unicorn at sea in the Indian Ocean with a Swordfish of 818 squadron on deck.

Unicorn *manoeuvring with tugs at Freemantle.*

Unicorn sailed for Sydney on 29 January 1945 in company with the cruiser *Sussex*, crossing "the line" again on 31 January. She arrived in Fremantle, Western Australia on 5 February for a fuelling stop, having just missed a Typhoon that caused a considerable amount of damage ashore. She moved on quickly and arrived in Sydney with her important cargo of aircraft on 12 February. As the only efficient aircraft support facility in the BPF at the time, *Unicorn's* Aircraft Repair Division was hard pressed to modify and prepare aircraft for issue to the fleet squadrons. She also had to take on board all the available stores to support the whole range of aircraft in the BPF, not all of which had been available in Ceylon, contrary to the planner's belief.

On 28 February 1945 *Unicorn* sailed for Manus in the Admiralty Islands carrying the reserve aircraft pool for the BPF's operational work up. Ferrying aircraft between the carriers by lighter proved to be difficult in the swell encountered during this phase of activity and

a number of aircraft were damaged. One Seafire was lost over the side during a transfer in rough conditions when a sling broke. Several of the lighter's crew were hurt but none seriously. On 27 March she arrived at San Pedro Bay in Leyte Gulf which was to act as the intermediate base for the BPF's replenishment between the two phases of Operation "Iceberg". By this stage she had to support four fleet carriers in action, *Illustrious*, *Victorious*, *Indomitable* and *Indefatigable*. After the first phase *Formidable* arrived to relieve *Illustrious* and so, briefly, activities in five ships had to be supported as aircraft and stores were transferred prior to *Illustrious'* departure for Australia and the UK. While this large force was anchored together from 23 April onwards, *Unicorn's* two aircraft lighters had to work a non-stop day and night ferry service carrying aircraft between the carriers and between herself and the ferry and replenishment carriers for over seven days. Fortunately, the sea was much calmer than it had been off Manus but the effort was worthy of note and Admiral Sir Bernard Rawlings, Second-in-Command of the BPF signalled his appreciation of the effort. As the principal element of the Air Train during this stage of operations, **Unicorn** was responsible for providing most of the replacement aircraft that were made available to the fleet carriers.

At the end of operations in support of the Okinawa landings, the BPF and its Fleet Train withdrew to the main base in Sydney for battle damage repairs and replenishment. **Unicorn** left the anchorage at Leyte Gulf on 22 May and arrived in Sydney on 1 June. She spent six days taking on aircraft stores before sailing for Brisbane on 6 June. Once there she was docked to have her underwater fittings checked and to have her bottom cleaned and painted. Whilst there she embarked a load of replacement aircraft and sailed for Manus. She arrived on 22 July joining **Pioneer** and **Deer Sound** to form an expanded and improved Air Train in support of BPF operations against the Japanese mainland. **Pioneer** had been fitted out to

specialise in work on Corsair and Avenger aircraft allowing **Unicorn** to concentrate mainly on the other three types.

Unicorn was with the Air Train at Manus on VJ Day. The end of the war was celebrated by "Splicing the Mainbrace" and, despite the tropical heat, by the provision of a special dinner. The menu included tomato soup, roast turkey with peas and roast potatoes and rich plum pudding! The end of hostilities brought a change of activity and **Unicorn** was used to ferry men and equipment back to the main base in Australia. While she did so her own Aircraft Repair Department was landed to the TAMY to make more space available on board. She was in Brisbane to unload aircraft on 23 September and then returned to Manus to evacuate the outposts on Ponam and Pityilu Islands, arriving on 6 October and leaving on 9 October. Brisbane was used as her main port because of its proximity to the TAMY, where aircraft that were now "war surplus" were to be concentrated. A last run to close down the air station on Ponam was carried out later in October,

Unicorn *at Manus in 1945.*

Unicorn alongside in Fremantle, Western Australia, on her way from Ceylon to Sydney.

arriving on the 24th and sailing on 31 October, this time to Sydney where she arrived on 6 November. *Unicorn* had been away from the UK since December 1943 with substantially the same ship's company and so she was a strong candidate for an early return to the UK, leaving *Pioneer* as the BPF's maintenance carrier on station. She landed stores and equipment for use by the reduced BPF that was to remain in being.

During this wartime commission, *Unicorn*'s Aircraft Repair Division worked on 626 aircraft and 283 aircraft engines. Aircraft types included Albacores, Fulmars, Sea Hurricanes, Seafires, Swordfish, Walrus, Barracudas, Avengers, Corsairs, Hellcats, Fireflies, Vengeances and Martinets. The latter two types were Fleet Requirement Unit types ferried between air stations. In the same period, the ship's company consumed 764,998 pounds of bread; 85,189 pints of rum; 204,822 pounds of sugar; 28,391 pounds of tea; 353,893 eggs and 276,901 tins of milk.

The highest recorded air temperature was 110°F in Bombay and the highest sea water temperature 90°F in Leyte Gulf.

Unicorn arrived back in the UK at Devonport Dockyard in January 1946. Her ship's company paid off and she joined the Reserve Fleet moored in the River Tamar. For a while she was close to *Renown*, the Royal Navy's last battle cruiser before being recommissioned in 1949 to ferry aircraft, stores and support equipment to the Far East in support of *Triumph*, the aircraft carrier on station. By then the BPF had been renamed as the Far East Fleet (FEF) with its main base at Singapore and a secondary base at Hong Kong. She sailed from Devonport on 22 September 1949 with a load of Seafire 47 and Firefly 1 aircraft and a considerable outfit of stores.

When the Communist North Korean forces invaded South Korea on 25 June 1950, *Unicorn* was in Singapore Naval Base disembarking aircraft, stores

Unicorn moored in Leyte Gulf with replacement aircraft on deck.

and the majority of her air maintenance personnel to RNAS Sembawang. It was intended that she should return to the UK after a short refit and de-store into reserve again. *Triumph* was in Japanese waters with the bulk of the FEF for exercises with the US Seventh Fleet. With the American carriers, she went into action on 3 July 1950 and it was clear that she would need air logistic support on a considerable scale if the FEF were to remain effective. The creation of the BPF was a recent memory and it was clear that the lessons learnt applied directly to the new conflict. *Unicorn* was ordered to remain in the FEF as the nucleus of an Air Train to support the operational carriers. She re-embarked aircraft and stores while consideration was given to the best way of employing her. Two alternatives were considered for the Air Train. *Unicorn* could operate as an aircraft repair ship moored at a forward base as she had done at Leyte Gulf and Manus in 1945 or, alternatively, she could land her Aircraft Repair Department, workshop equipment and stores to RNAS Sembawang and operate as a replenishment carrier. The latter alternative was considered the more efficient and was adopted. She retained a light repair and maintenance capability.

Unicorn sailed from Singapore on 11 July, initially for Okinawa but then for Sasebo, which was to be used as a Commonwealth naval base throughout the Korean War. She arrived on 20 July and transferred seven Seafires and five Fireflies to *Triumph*. The importance of such a ship to the war effort was, by then, obvious and she began a series of voyages to ferry aircraft, stores and even troops to the war zone. As in the Pacific War, Britain faced the problem of supporting a main base many thousands of miles from the UK which in turn had to support a forward base over a thousand miles distant that, in turn, supported the operational fleet. The light fleet carrier *Warrior* was recommissioned to act as a ferry carrier moving aircraft and personnel from the UK to the Far East. During August 1950, *Unicorn* was loaded with stores as diverse as aircraft engines, ammunition, rum and flour in addition to aircraft for onward shipment to Hong Kong. She sailed from Hong Kong for Sasebo on 18 August but was recalled within hours to embark men of the First Battalion the Middlesex Regiment and the Headquarters of 27 Infantry

Brigade for service in Korea. The cruiser **Ceylon** carried men of the First Battalion the Argyle and Sutherland Highlanders and the two ships entered the UN port of Pusan, with **Unicorn** in the lead, to land them on 29 August. They were the first British troops to arrive in Korea and most of their vehicles had been tightly packed into **Unicorn's** lower hangar, a feat few other warships could have equalled. She moved to Sasebo on 30 August to pass stores to **Triumph** and then sailed on 2 September to carry out the refit that had been planned for June in Singapore. While she was there, **Theseus** with an air group of Sea Furies and later marks of Firefly replaced **Triumph** on station. **Unicorn** sailed north again on 2 December on the first of what was to become a reg-

ular series of runs with over 400 troops embarked in addition to aircraft, stores and military equipment. As in the BPF, her deck was used by pilots who were new to the fleet for deck landing practice so that they could work up to operational efficiency without the front line carrier having to alter its operational programme.

Among the more unusual cargoes she carried in March 1951 were the Meteor jet fighters of 77 Squadron RAAF that had been brought to Singapore in **Warrior**. She delivered them to Iwakuni on 22 March. By then, Iwakuni had a small RN Aircraft Holding Unit (AHU) and fulfilled many of the functions that RNAS Ponam had fulfilled in the Admiralty Islands in 1945, albeit on a smaller scale. The airfield

*An Avenger aircraft leaving **Unicorn** at Manus. Note how small the lighter was and how easily a swell could make such transfers hazardous.*

was the other side of Hiroshima Bay from the dockyard at Kure and was administered by the RAAF under a Group Captain. It had a number of lodger units in addition to 77 Squadron including USAF B-25 bombers, USN Neptunes and a RAF Sunderland Flight. It was a staging post for the US Military Air Transport Service, RAF Transport Command and QANTAS. Like the MONABs before it, the AHU started with primitive facilities making an office out of engine crates and a workshop on the back of a three-ton lorry. It comprised a single officer, initially Lieutenant Foster, one Chief Aircraft Artificer, four Petty Officers and twenty sailors. It was responsible for 'holding' up to 24 replacement aircraft, of which two had to be at twenty four hours' notice for operational use. Their workload varied from intense when *Unicorn* unloaded aircraft or the operational carrier took them on board to dull when both were not present. During the quiet periods they turned to with a will

to help the other lodger units and were, in turn, helped by them.

For three months in the spring of 1951, *Unicorn* acted as an accommodation ship in Sasebo before returning to ferry runs between Singapore, Hong Kong and Japan from June. In addition to the usual Sea Furies and Fireflies, she carried Army Air Corps Austers, RAF Vampires for Hong Kong and further batches of Meteor fighters for 77 squadron RAAF at Iwakuni and literally hundreds of military passengers into the war zone. She was "adopted" by the Middlesex Regiment after a continued close association. She continued to perform tasks that were unusual for a carrier. On 22 September 1951 a salvage party from the ship rescued two aircraft that had been stranded at Paengyong-do from *Glory*, using a "borrowed" USN landing craft from which they were winched on board. As if that was not enough, she went on to cross the thirty-eighth parallel and bombard

Even a Hellcat had little room to spare on the lighter. This one is being taken ashore for a test flight at Pityilu Island.

Unicorn in dry dock at Brisbane.   *(Royal Australian Navy)*

North Korean huts used by coast watchers at Chopekki Point. At the time of writing she remains the only aircraft carrier to have carried out a shore bombardment under wartime conditions. The shoot was very successful. In a series of short visits between Japanese ports, ***Unicorn*** assisted in the handover of operational duties from ***Glory*** to HMAS ***Sydney*** in late September.

Despite her height, ***Unicorn*** tended to use the Shimonoseki Strait on passage between Sasebo and Iwakuni. Despite the usual careful checks on the state of the tide, she struck the power lines stretching from Honshu to Kyushu on 2 October because they were covered in snow and sagging lower than expected in the extremely cold weather. It took some weeks to replace the lines and the ship tended to steam to the south of Kyushu after that. Later in the month she had to sail from Sasebo to ride out Hurricane Ruth. She avoided the centre and rode out the storm at sea encountering winds gusting to 100 knots and waves up to 50 feet high.

After this eventful period in the war zone she returned to Singapore, via Hong Kong. Her ship's company had left the UK two years previously, expecting to be away for less than a year. The ship's role was so important that they were replaced on station with a new ship's company, which steamed the ferry carrier ***Warrior*** out to Singapore. They took over ***Unicorn*** by 24 November 1951 and the old ship's company steamed ***Warrior*** back to the UK. The ship was taken in hand for a refit in Singapore Dockyard, which lasted until 20 January 1952.

Unicorn in the River Tamar as part of the Devonport Reserve Fleet in 1948. The ship in the foreground is the battle-cruiser *Renown* carrying out its last sunset ceremony.

On her return to ferrying duties she carried RAF aircraft to Hong Kong and RN and RAAF aircraft into the war zone. In Hong Kong she assisted in the handover of operational duties from *Sydney* to *Glory* on 2 February. On 7 February she fired a 56 gun salute, one gun a minute for every year of the late King George VI's life. On the following day, she fired a 21 gun salute to mark the Accession of Her Majesty Queen Elizabeth II. A memorial service for the late king was held on the quarterdeck, attended by a number of senior allied officers. In March she took part in Exercise Vortex off Hong Kong, playing the part of a light fleet carrier providing useful deck landing experience for pilots who were new to the Far East Station. In April the presentation of the Regimental March and a special Order of the Day from the Regiment's colonel marked the close association with the Middlesex Regiment. Both were mounted on the quarterdeck next to the ship's battle honours. To the best of the Captain's knowledge, only two other British 'ships' had been similarly honoured by regiments, the battleship *Vanguard* and the gunnery school at Whale Island - HMS *Excellent*. *Unicorn*'s routine ferry trips continued until July when she operated as a spare deck during strike operations against North Korea by *Ocean* escorted by HMCS *Nootka* and HMAS *Bataan*. This allowed a Firefly to land on with a fuel leak and be replaced rather than interrupting the strike carrier's deck cycle, a successful use of *Unicorn* that was to be repeated several times before the war ended. On 27 July she returned to Singapore where she transferred "war-weary" aircraft to *Vengeance* for passage to the UK.

On 9 August *Unicorn* sailed for Iwakuni with a deck load of Meteors for 77 Squadron and her hangars full of replacement naval aircraft. She carried out another war patrol with *Ocean* from 1 September, borrowing four pilots from the light fleet carrier to fly Combat Air Patrols (CAP) over the fleet with Sea Furies. In October she completed a self-maintenance period and embarked the First Sea Lord, Admiral Sir Rhoderick McGrigor and the C-in-C Far East Station for a visit to Commonwealth forces in Japan. After this she ferried men and material between Singapore, Hong Kong,

Unicorn entering Grand Harbour, Malta.

Unicorn *transferring aircraft and stores to **Ocean** at Kure during the Korean War.*

Pusan and Kure before returning to Singapore on 15 December 1952 for a docking and refit. The ship's company moved ashore into the barracks, HMS **Terror**, with the Air Department moving ashore to RNAS Sembawang. On completion of the refit, she re-stored and moored in Singapore Roads with **Glory** and a number of other ships of the Far East Fleet for celebrations to mark the Coronation of HM Queen Elizabeth II. After a period alongside the Dockyard, **Unicorn** sailed for Japan, via Hong Kong, on 17 July 1953 with a load of Sea Furies and Fireflies that had been prepared for operational service at RNAS Sembawang.

Whilst on passage from Hong Kong to Kure on 26 July, fifty miles from Ockseu Island, **Unicorn** intercepted a signal from SS **Inchkilda** saying that she was being attacked by gunboats. **Unicorn** immediately went to her aid and closed the scene at high speed with all armament manned. She circled the gunboats at less than 3,000 yards, training her medium and close range guns on them. The sight was too much for the pirates

who re-boarded their vessels and fled to the west. **Inchkilda** was returned to her master and went on her way little the worse.

A day later, on 27 July 1953, the Armistice that ended fighting in the Korean War was finally signed. **Unicorn** sailed for a final operational patrol in company with **Ocean** on 30 July to ensure that the terms of the cease-fire were being complied with. She returned to Sasebo on 12 August but carried out one more patrol between 25 and 29 August. She left Kure on 31 August and had to take avoiding action around Hurricane Susan after leaving Hong Kong en route for Singapore. After four years away from home and two separate commissions on station, **Unicorn** was released from the Far East Station for the passage back to the UK on 15 October 1953. She had delivered a remarkable performance, having steamed 130,000 miles and spent over 500 days at sea. In addition to handling over 600 aircraft, her primary function, she had delivered more than 6,000 troops into the war zone together with bulk shipments of stores, ammunition and vehicles. In the dark days of August 1950 she had carried the first British troops into Pusan. In addition to doing so well in her designed role she had operated as an operational carrier and as training 'deck' for new pilots. Unlike any other carrier she had carried out a shore bombardment of enemy forces under wartime conditions, foiled an attack on a merchant ship by pirates and formed such close links with an infantry Regiment that she was adopted as part of it by the colonel!

Unicorn arrived back in Devonport on 17 November 1953 and rejoined the reserve fleet in the River Tamar. She was re-designated as a ferry carrier and given the new pennant number A 195. In consequence, some of her workshop equipment was removed for use in naval air yards ashore but she was partially manned so that she could, if necessary, be returned to operational service at short notice. Her usefulness in the Korean conflict had led to plans to include a replenishment carrier as a permanent feature

of the post-war fleet. *Unicorn* was the most capable ship to retain and plans were prepared for her modernisation in 1951. These included the fitting of a steam catapult with a 103 foot stroke and strengthening the flight deck to launch 25,000lb aircraft and recover 22,000lb aircraft. A new crane capable of lifting the third generation jets then under development was specified. Both hangars were relatively low and thought was given to creating a single high hangar out of the two, along the lines of the conversion being prepared for the fleet carriers *Indefatigable* and *Implacable*. Once the enormous cost of such a scheme was understood, however, it was not included in the plan. In October 1951 it was intended to take *Unicorn* in hand for modernisation in July 1954. However, it was decided in July 1952 not to proceed as, by then, the modernisation of *Victorious* was demonstrating the high cost of such work. To be viable operating the new generation of jets, *Unicorn* would have needed a fully angled flight deck in addi-

Unicorn at sea off Korea. The overhang at the rear of the flight deck and the opening into the hangar beneath it are clear in this view.

tion to the other work. The Admiralty came to the conclusion that money would be better spent fitting angled decks to the new fleet and light fleet carriers coming into service and she stayed in reserve.

In March 1957 she was reduced to extended reserve with no further maintenance and in 1958 she was placed on the disposal list. She was sold for scrap to the firm of Arnott Young and towed from Devonport in June 1959. She arrived at Dalmuir to be stripped out on 15 June 1959 with the hull eventually being scrapped at Troon in 1960.

Technical Specifications

Machinery:	2-shaft Parsons geared turbines; 4 Admiralty 3-drum boilers; 40,000 shp = 24 knots.
Displacement:	14,750 tons standard; 20,300 tons deep load
Dimensions:	640 ft overall x 90 ft max beam x 24 ft 10 in max draught.
Gun armament:	4 twin 4 inch QF Mk 16 HA (8); 4 quadruple 2-pdr (16); 5 twin 20 mm Oerlikon (10); 6 single 20 mm Oerlikon (6); 4 single 3 pdr saluting guns.
Furnace fuel:	3,000 tons FFO.
Endurance:	7,500 miles @ 20 knots.
Complement:	1,200 with aircraft repair department.
Protection:	2 inch plated flight deck; 2 inch magazine crowns; 4 inch to 4.5 inch magazine sides; 1 inch NC lift platforms; 1.25 inch internal anti-torpedo bulkhead.
Flight deck:	640 x 90 feet armoured steel.
Arrester wires:	6 x 20,000lb @ 60 knots; 1 barrier.
Hangars:	Upper - 324 ft x 65 ft x 16 ft 6 inch. Lower - 360 ft x 62 ft x 16 ft 6 inch.
Catapult:	One BH 3; 12,500lb @ 66 knots.
Lifts:	Forward - 46 ft long x 33 ft wide. Aft - 46 ft long x 24 ft wide. Both 20,000lb with a 46-second cycle.
Aircraft:	35 as an operational carrier. 50 or more as a ferry carrier. About 24 under repair.

Sources:

• Aircraft Carriers of the Royal and Commonwealth Navies by David Hobbs. Published by Greenhill Books, London, 1996.
• Aircraft Carriers by David Brown. Published by MacDonald and Jane's, London, 1997.
• HMS *Unicorn* Commission Book 1945, printed by Langlea Printery Pty Ltd, Sydney, in the Author's Collection.

Chapter Four

HMS PIONEER

HMS *Pioneer* passing under Sydney Harbour Bridge in May 1945

BACKGROUND

The urgent need to provide aircraft maintenance facilities afloat to support the British Pacific Fleet led to the conversion of two light fleet carriers into aircraft maintenance ships before their completion. These each provided roughly half the capability of *Unicorn* in less time than it would have taken to build a new ship. With the large number of light fleet carrier hulls under construction, the increased support capability they were to provide more than outweighed the theoretical loss of operational capability. Indeed, by 1944 there were considerable doubts about the Royal Navy's ability to provide air groups for all

the new carriers if the war continued, as expected, into 1946. Although capable of carrying out a wide range of tasks, the modified ships were intended primarily as aircraft maintenance and repair ships. Other ships, with merchant hulls, were under construction for the engine and component repair tasks.

The first of the two Colossus class light fleet carrier conversions to be completed was begun as *Mars*. She was laid down by Vickers-Armstrong at their Barrow-in-Furness shipyard on 2 December 1942 and launched on 20 May 1943. After the decision to change her role, her name was changed to *Pioneer*.

The aircraft metal repair shop.

Air ordnance ratings working on Browning machine guns in the Ordnance Workshop.

The Battery Charging Room. Note the coffee mug in the right foreground.

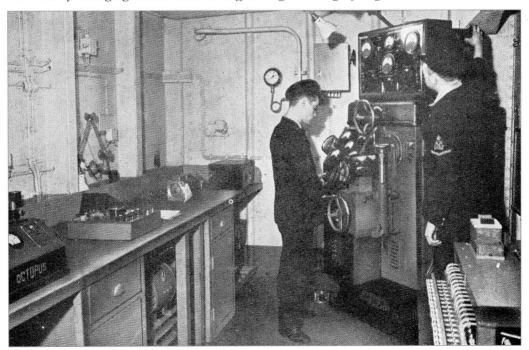

The Electrical Repair Shop.

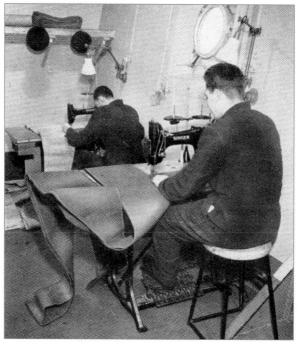

The Fabric Workers Shop.

The key factor in the revised design was the provision of the largest possible maintenance facilities in the minimum time optimising the available hull volume. It was decided not to retain aircraft operating equipment and to reduce the armament in order to make room for larger workshops and stores. This meant that, unlike *Unicorn*, aircraft could not be flown on and off and would have to be craned onto the upper deck from lighters. The light anti-aircraft armament did not need to be mounted on sponsons to clear the deck and was mounted on the upper deck, giving these ships cleaner lines than their half sisters. The opportunity was taken to build extra structure onto the former flight deck, used for engine storage, oxygen production offices and a cinema.

SERVICE WITH THE BRITISH PACIFIC FLEET

Pioneer completed on 8 February 1945 and commissioned at Barrow-in-Furness. She embarked her Aircraft Repair Department and, after a short work-up, sailed from the Clyde for Australia on 30 March 1945. She was on passage in April and arrived in Sydney on 13 May 1945. On 8 June 1945 she was in Sydney with *Unicorn* and *Deer Sound*, flying the broad pennant of the Commodore Air Train, Commodore H S Murray-Smith RN, *Pioneer's* Commanding Officer.

She sailed for Seeadler Harbour on the northern coast of Manus Island, the largest of the Admiralty Islands, where she arrived with the remainder of the Air Train on 21 June. Her primary task was to establish the RN Forward Aircraft Pool at the US Naval Air Station on Pityilu Island and this was achieved by 11 July 1945. *Pioneer* was joined at Manus by the only other units of the Air Train to see service before the war ended. These included *Deer Sound*, which

arrived on 24 June followed by *Unicorn* on 21 July. The Air Stores Issuing Ship (ASIS) RFA *Fort Langley* arrived direct from the builder in Canada during July and the ASIS RFA *Fort Colville* joined in early August. During this last phase of operations against Japan the Air Train provided the BPF with 28 aircraft at Manus to bring it up to full strength before it sailed to the north and 155 aircraft to replenishment carriers in seven replenishment loads. Of these 17 aircraft failed to reach the fleet before the armistice and were returned. 18 aircraft from the previous load were not required and were also returned. 52 unserviceable aircraft were returned to the Air Train at Manus in replenishment carriers.

Before *Unicorn* arrived, *Pioneer's* two aircraft lighters were the only means of moving aircraft over the three-mile haul between the fleet anchorage and Pityilu and they ran virtually non-stop. A third, unserviceable, lighter had been embarked in Sydney and,

after a great deal of work, this was brought into use in late July. Even with *Unicorn's* two lighters the number was still insufficient and USN lighters capable of carrying up to 4 aircraft had, frequently, to be borrowed.

While at Manus, *Pioneer* repaired 24 aircraft in eight weeks and, after ground running them, lightered them ashore to the FAP on Pityilu for test flight. Both she and *Unicorn* maintained small flight test parties with the FAP. These were responsible for bringing the aircraft repaired in their respective ships up to operational readiness before transferring them to the pool. Remarkably, however, it was not possible to swing the compasses as neither ship carried an observer for the task. *Pioneer* was at Manus when the Japanese surrendered on 15 August 1945 and remained there until early September.

Among the first priorities after the surrender was the re-occupation of the Crown Colony of Hong Kong.

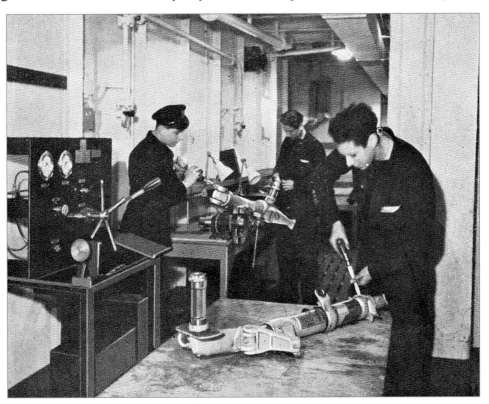

The Hydraulic and Oleo Repair Shop.

*The distinctive crane on the forward part of **Pioneer's** upper deck lifting an aircraft lighter onto its stowage prior to sailing*

A mobile crane or "Jumbo" lowering a crated component into a lift well.

*The Smiths and Welders'
Shop.*

The Wireless Test Room and Store.

HMS *Pioneer* in Sydney Harbour. Note the standard crane aft of the Island and the more distictive crane on the forward part of the upper deck. The aircraft on deck are Avengers and Corsairs with a single DUKW amphibious vehicle near the Island.   (Royal Australian Navy)

HMS *Pioneer* returning to Sydney from Hong Kong in Decemeber 1945. She took passage via Bougainville and picked up Australian troops to return them home, many of them can be seen on the upper deck forward of the island. Peacetime standards have returned and hands, in their whites, are fallen in on the upper deck for Procedure "Alpha". The aircraft on deck are Corsairs and Avengers.

The 11th Aircraft Carrier Squadron under Rear Admiral C H J Harcourt left Sydney on 15 August comprising the flagship **Indomitable**, **Venerable** with the cruiser **Swiftsure**, with orders to move to Hong Kong via Leyte Gulf. After flying off aircraft to fly low over the city and destroy enemy "suicide boats" on Lamma Island off Aberdeen, the warships entered Hong Kong harbour on 30 August. Armed parties to restore order were landed from 1 September and Admiral Harcourt formally accepted the Japanese surrender. Parties of sailors restored power, telephones, trains, buses and even formed mounted patrols.

With their large technical staffs, maintenance and repair ships of the Fleet Train were deployed to Hong Kong to help with the work of restoration. **Pioneer** was there on 1 October 1945 having arrived in late September. After a return to Manus, she was at Hong Kong again in late November after which she sailed for Sydney. She was at sea on 17 December 1945.

Her sister ship **Perseus** arrived in Sydney on 21 December and hoisted the broad pennant of COMAT since, with the run-down of the BPF only one maintenance carrier was required on station. After a short defect rectification period, **Pioneer** sailed for Singapore and the UK on 17 February 1946. On arrival, she was immediately reduced to reserve. She was never brought forward again for operational use, despite being re-designated as a ferry carrier in June 1953. After being placed on the Disposal List, she was sold to T W Ward in September 1954 and towed to Inverkeithing where she was broken up for scrap.

Technical Specifications

Machinery:	2-shaft Parsons single-reduction geared turbines; 4 Admiralty 3-drum boilers; 40,000 shp = 24.5 knots.
Displacement:	12,265 tons standard; 16,500 tons deep load.
Dimensions:	695 ft overall x 80 ft 4 in max beam x 23 ft max draught.
Gun armament:	6 quadruple 2-pdr (24); 19 single 40mm Bofors (19).
Furnace Fuel:	3,196 tons FFO.
Endurance:	8,500 miles @ 11 knots.
Complement:	1,076 with Aircraft maintenance Department.
Protection:	No armour. Machinery units built in echelon.
Flight deck:	Space for parking and engine runs on the upper deck. Capable of operating helicopters.
Arrester wires:	None.
Hangar:	275 ft x 52 ft x 17 ft 6 in.
Catapult:	None.
Lifts:	Forward - 45 ft long x 34 ft wide. Aft - 45 ft long x 35 ft wide. Both 15,000lb.
Aircraft:	Up to 60 could be ferried. About 20 under repair.
Aircraft fuel:	98,600 gallons AVGAS.

Sources:

- Aircraft Carriers of the Royal and Commonwealth Navies by David Hobbs. Published by Greenhill Books, London, 1996.
- Engineering in the Royal Navy reprinted from the Machine Tool Engineering Journal, June 1945.
- Report on the organisation of the Flag Officer Nval Air Parties in the Archive of the Fleet Air Arm Museum.
- HMS *Pioneer* Commission Book 1945 in the Author's Collection.

Chapter Five

HMS PERSEUS

HMS *Perseus* in Sydney Harbour in 1946.   *(Royal Australian Navy)*

BACKGROUND

The second of the light fleet carriers to be converted into an aircraft maintenance ship was laid down as *Edgar* on 1 June 1942 at Vickers-Armstrong's Walker Naval Yard at Newcastle-upon-Tyne. She was launched on 26 March 1943 after which she was converted for the new role and renamed *Perseus*. She differed only in detail from her sister ship *Pioneer*, the most obvious external variation being the different type of crane on the former flight deck forward.

Perseus was too late to see war service and did not complete until 19 October 1945. She commissioned in Newcastle on the same day and arrived in Portsmouth on 24 October. She sailed for the Far East on 17 November, stopping briefly in Singapore on 8 December and arrived in Sydney on 21 December. Once there, her commanding officer assumed the

duties of COMAT although by that stage the Air Train was in the process of running down. The Commodore's broad pendant was struck on 28 February 1946 marking the formal end of the force. *Perseus* left Sydney on 22 March for a brief visit to Melbourne and then sailed for the UK, via Ceylon and the Mediterranean, on 26 March. She carried a load of aircraft from the BPF to return to the Naval Aircraft Repair Organisation in the UK for further use. She arrived at Rosyth Dockyard on 17 May 1946 where she was reduced to reserve after her brief operational life.

Unlike her sister ship *Pioneer*, however, *Perseus* was to see further important service that would generate considerable international interest. In 1936 an engineer named Colin Mitchell, then working for the firm of MacTaggart, Scott and Co, conceived the idea

The Order of the Bath - Crossing the Line Ceremony on the upper deck on passage to Australia.

The prototype BXS 1 steam catapult was installed on the former upper deck under a false flight deck from which deadloads and aircraft were launched. A concrete weight is seen here being launched early in the trials programme.

Wheeled deadload shot into the Dockyard basin at Rosyth. Note the wire strop falling away.

British deadloads were given names, this is "Noah" after a successful catapult shot on 14 November 1950.

of a "slotted cylinder" catapult in which the piston that drove the catapult shuttle was driven directly by steam from the ship's boilers. Contemporary hydraulic catapults employed pistons that transmitted power to the shuttle by a series of sheaves and pulleys, losing a great deal of energy in the process. The Admiralty was interested but with no requirement to exceed the power of the hydraulic catapult at the time and insufficient money to build a speculative prototype the idea lapsed although Mitchell took out a patent in 1938. On the outbreak of war he was given a commission in the RNR and joined the Department of the Engineer in Chief at the Admiralty.

By 1945 it was apparent that the hydraulic catapult had reached the end of its development potential. Mitchell took a keen interest in reports of German catapults recently captured by allied troops in France and arranged to visit one in November 1944. He returned with sufficient material to build a working slotted

cylinder catapult, powered by cordite, at Shoeburyness. With this he was able to stimulate interest in his original steam powered concept and the Admiralty took the decision to adopt the steam catapult in 1946. A test unit, the BXS 1 was produced for installation in a ship to carry out sea trials.

The BXS 1 was installed in *Perseus* during a special refit in 1950. It was fitted in a superstructure running from the bow to a point level with the after end of the island structure on top of the upper deck (the original flight deck). It necessitated the removal of the box like structure to port of the island but the structure aft containing the engine store and oxygen plant was retained. A series of sea trials were carried out, in conditions of great secrecy, during which 1,560 catapult launches were achieved. Over 1,000 of these were wheeled deadloads, the weight of which could be carefully measured, controlled and steadily increased. Once confidence was established, unmanned aircraft were

The second phase of testing - VP 460, a Seafire FR 47, being loaded by crane onto the catapult from the dockside on 8 May 1951.

VP 460 on the catapult seconds before launch.

launched with the outer wings removed so that, in theory, they would not fly. Most of these were Seafires and Sea Hornets, which were surplus to operational requirements. Some of these were very light and flew surprisingly well, giving rise to hair raising legends of aircraft heading towards the coast before they ditched. Finally manned launches were carried out by every type of carrier-borne aircraft in service with the Royal Navy including jets. Because *Perseus* could only launch, but not recover aircraft, the operational types, like the deadloads and pilotless aircraft before them, had to be craned on board while the ship was alongside in a dockyard.

The USN had followed the development of the steam catapult with a great deal of interest and on 31 December 1951 *Perseus* sailed from Rosyth for Philadelphia in the USA where she demonstrated the new equipment. She arrived on 14 January and 'shots' with USN deadloads preceded live launches with operational types. Interestingly USN deadloads were given six digit numbers to identify them whereas

British deadloads were always given names such as "Flossy". In all, a total of 127 British and American piloted launches were made before the trials were finally completed. *Perseus* sailed from Philadelphia on 10 March 1952 and arrived back in Portsmouth Dockyard on 21 March. She paid off into dockyard hands and the experimental catapult was stripped out. It had proved so successful that the RN and USN immediately adopted it and, eventually, so did every navy that operated conventional fixed-wing aircraft from carrier decks including those of Argentina, Australia, Brazil, Canada, France, Holland and India. While in Portsmouth, *Perseus* had all her remaining maintenance equipment and prototype catapult equipment removed and she recommissioned as a ferry carrier. With no fixed wing aircraft and a large, unobstructed flight deck, she was able to operate helicopters and became the Royal Navy's first dedicated helicopter carrier. On 10 December 1952 she sailed for the Far East with 848 Naval Air Squadron embarked for service in Malaya. Having disembarked them to

VP 460 seconds after launch. Some Seafires flew surprisingly well, despite the removal of the outer wings.

A number of different types were catapulted, a Barracuda being loaded onto the catapult structure by "Jumbo" the mobile crane.

A short Sturgeon being prepared for launch.

Once the new catapult was deemed to be safe, manned aircraft were launched. The pilot of firefly is seen climbing into his aircraft after it has been positioned on the catapult.

Fireflies and Avengers lined up on deck for a multiple launch.

RNAS Sembawang in Singapore on 8 January 1953 she sailed for Portsmouth on 15 January, arriving on 11 February 1953. Like other carriers, she carried RN drafts and troops to the Far East.

In March she embarked 200 officers and men of the RNR for sea training and sailed for Norfolk, Virginia on the 6th. She arrived on 16 March and embarked the first consignment of the 100 Grumman Avenger aircraft allocated to the RN under the Mutual Defence Assistance Programme (MDAP). She sailed for the UK on 18 March via a brief fuelling stop at Bermuda on 20 March. *Perseus* arrived in the Clyde on 30 March to offload the aircraft to the Aircraft Holding Unit (AHU) at RNAS Abbotsinch and returned to Portsmouth on 2 April. She sailed on 20 April for a further ferry trip to collect the balance of the Avengers, arriving at Norfolk on 29 April and sailing on 4 May 1953. After stops at Bermuda and the Clyde again, she returned to Portsmouth on 18 May. While there she

was officially re-designated as a ferry carrier. Her flight deck was covered in seating galleries from which VIPs and the press were able to watch the Coronation Review of the Fleet at Spithead in June 1953, another unusual use for a an aircraft carrier! After the seating was removed she sailed from Portsmouth on 17 August 1953 for a trooping run ferrying reserve aircraft, personnel and stores to the Far East. She arrived in Singapore on 23 September and returned to Portsmouth on 9 November 1953.

On 20 January 1954 she became a helicopter carrier again and embarked the Sikorsky Whirlwind HAS 22 helicopters of 706 Naval Air Squadron. She sailed with them for sea trials with the new anti-submarine helicopters to see if they were viable. She was based in Northern Ireland and operated out of Belfast and Bangor with ships of the Joint Anti-Submarine School (JASS) based at Londonderry. The trials were so successful that 706, a second-line squadron normally

USN dockyard staff position a deadweight for launch in Philadelphia Navy Yard during 1952.

US Navy Douglas Skyraider at full power about to be catapulted.

US Navy McDonnell Banshee on the catapult.....

......US Navy Piasecki HUP 1 helicopter landing on **Perseus** during sea trials off Philadelphia in March 1952".

Perseus during the Coronation Review of the Fleet at Spithead in June 1953 with seating galleries erected on the flight deck.

based ashore, was redesignated as a front line unit and re-numbered as 845 Naval Air Squadron on 15 March 1954. The new squadron embarked in *Perseus* on 21 April 1954 for passage to the Mediterranean and it disembarked to RNAS Hal Far in Malta on 28 April, subsequently seeing service in a number of Mediterranean Fleet carriers including *Eagle*, *Centaur* and *Albion*. *Perseus* herself continued to the Far East with relief supplies for Korea. She arrived in Singapore Naval Base on 25 May to unload them and then sailed to return to the UK on 5 June. She arrived in Portsmouth on 12 July 1954 and was then taken to Rosyth by a skeleton ship's company to be reduced to reserve. She

was relieved by *Glory* in the ferry role from August 1954.

The Admiralty planned to convert *Perseus* into a submarine depot ship and she was towed to Belfast in 1955 for work to start. However, the notorious 1957 Defence Review reduced the size of the future fleet and the number of projected submarine depot ships was cut back from three to two. Work on *Perseus* was abandoned, she was reduced to extended reserve and towed to the Gareloch to await disposal. In May 1958 she was sold to Smith and Houston for scrap and towed to Port Glasgow to be broken up

Technical Specifications

As per HMS *Pioneer* (Page 73)

Sources:

- Aircraft Carriers of the Royal and Commonwealth Navies by David Hobbs. Published by Greenhill Books, London, 1996.
- Engineering in the Royal Navy reprinted from the Machine Tool Engineering Journal, June 1945.
- Diary of Steam Catapult trials in HMS *Perseus* in the Archive of the Fleet Air Arm Museum.
- HMS *Perseus* Commission Book 1946 in the Archive of the Fleet Air Arm Museum.

*A Whirlwind HAS 22 of 845 Naval Air Squadron embarking in **Perseus** in Portsmouth Dockyard on 21 April 1954. The deck is loaded with a variety of aircraft and vehicles for shipment to the Far East, including cocooned Sea Furies and, "Pusser's buses" and private cars".*

(Charles E Brown via RAF Museum)

Chapter Six

REPAIR SHIPS & FERRY CARRIERS

HMS Deer Sound *in Mossman Bay, Sydney in 1945.*

HMS DEER SOUND

A large construction programme was carried forward in Canada in 1944/45 intended to produce 23 maintenance ships based on mercantile hull designs. In addition to aircraft component repair ships these were intended to function as depot ships for landing craft, minesweepers, coastal forces and as medium maintenance and repair ships for the BPF. Five were incomplete at the end of hostilities and were completed after the war to the original mercantile design. Five ships were intended to form part of the Air Train, specialising in engine, instrument or general component repair.

Only one of the planned repair ships arrived in the BPF before the end of hostilities, the aircraft engine repair ship ***Deer Sound***. She had been built as the mercantile ***Port Quebec*** in 1939, requisitioned by the Admiralty and converted into an auxiliary minelayer. With the reduction in the need for minelayers as the war against Germany drew to a close she was available and already under Admiralty control. It was, thus, possible to convert her to the new role in advance of the ships under construction in Canada.

On completion of her role change she arrived in the Clyde on 1 January 1945 and prepared to deploy to the

Deer Sound *in Hong Kong harbour in September 1945.*

BPF. She left Colombo on 5 February. On 4 May 1945 she was at San Pedro Bay in Leyte Gulf with the Air Train. She was intended to support **Pioneer** with engine repair work but, limited by the shortage of spare parts and the low number of engines that found their way back to the air train for repair work, she never worked at full capacity. On 8 June she was back in the main base in Sydney with the remainder of the BPF and its Air Train. She sailed for Manus with **Pioneer** and was there, with the Air Train, on 9 July. She was still at Manus in early September but, with a number of other ships of the BPF, she deployed to Hong Kong to help restore the facilities in the Crown Colony to something approaching normal. With her workshops and technical ratings she was a considerable asset and remained in Hong Kong until December 1945 when she returned to Sydney before sailing for the UK. She returned to the UK in 1946 and, having been stripped of her workshops, she was returned to her original owners in 1947.

The other ships intended to act as aircraft component repair ships included **Beauly Firth**, **Moray Firth**, **Cuillin Sound** and **Holm Sound**. None of these played any significant part in the war, although **Beauly Firth** commissioned at Hebburn-on-Tyne on 11 June 1945 and arrived in Townsville in Queensland, Australia on 23 December and Brisbane on 30 December 1945. She returned to the UK carrying 800 tons of food for Britain as a gift from the people of Australia and paid off in Rosyth on 17 May 1946. **Holm Sound** also arrived in the Far East but the deployment of the other ships was eventually cancelled.

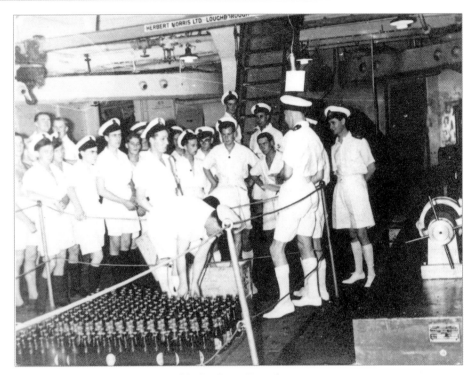

Holm Sound *Christmas Day 1945 - Beer Issue!*

Holm Sound *Sunday Divisions on the jetty in Fremantle.*

ESCORT, FERRY & REPLENISHMENT CARRIERS

The 30th Aircraft Carrier Squadron (30 ACS) administered all the escort carriers in the BPF that fulfilled the roles of ferry, replenishment and CAP carriers. By August 1945 it comprised HM Ships *Striker*, *Arbiter*, *Chaser*, *Ruler*, *Slinger*, *Speaker*, *Vindex* and *Reaper*.

Three other CVEs, *Activity*, *Begum* and *Fencer*, contributed to BPF operations as ferry carriers. Several other RN CVEs were lent to the USN for ferry operations in the Pacific Theatre of Operations.

HMS STRIKER

Striker was allocated to the BPF after service with the Home Fleet. She arrived in Sydney on 7 January 1945 and sailed ahead of the main force with a load of replacement aircraft on 7 March. She left Manus with 18 aircraft on 19 March and took up station with the replenishment group off the Sakashima Islands. 4 aircraft were flown off to the fleet on 25 March and 13 more on 28 March. *Speaker* provided a replacement Avenger crew to *Illustrious* on the same day and landed on 3 "flyable duds" for transport back to the Air Train at Leyte Gulf.

On 5 April 1945 she sailed from Leyte with a replenishment load of 14 aircraft. 12 of these were flown off to the fleet on 8 April and 4 "flyable duds" were recovered for the journey back to Leyte. On 6 May she was back in the replenishment area and flew off 15 aircraft for the BPF. She embarked 34 casualties from *Formidable* for passage to Leyte where they were transferred to a hospital ship. She was back later in May and transferred 14 replacement aircraft on 14 May and 6 on 15 May. On both days she recovered a single "flyable dud". The low number of "duds"

HMS Striker in Sydney harbour during February 1945.

recovered, compared with the number of replacements flown off to the BPF illustrate how the planners emphasis on repair, rather than erection of transported airframes in the main base, was not borne out by experience. She returned to Manus on 23 May 1945, after which she was used to ferry aircraft forward from Australia.

Striker became flagship of 30 ACS in July and prepared for operations with the Replenishment Group, Task Force 112, off the mainland of Japan in support of the BPF. She sailed from Manus in company with *Arbiter* on 9 July 1945. She flew off aircraft to the

fleet on 20 July and transferred her last 3 aircraft to *Speaker* on 27 July before returning to Manus. She arrived on 2 August and loaded with aircraft, sailing again for the RAS areas on 4 August. On 6 August she was ordered to return to Manus and then proceed to Sydney where she was loaded with stores and supplies for Hong Kong. She arrived in Hong Kong on 18 September and returned to Sydney in October. From there she was released by the BPF and made her way back to the UK, arriving back in the Clyde to de-store in December. She was returned to the USN at Norfolk Navy Yard in February 1946.

HMS ARBITER

HMS Arbiter.

Arbiter was allocated to the BPF in January 1945 after service with Western Approaches Command as a ferry carrier in the Atlantic. She sailed from the UK in March, with 1843 NAS embarked for passage with its Corsairs, and arrived in Sydney in May. After several runs ferrying aircraft to Manus, she sailed from Manus for the RAS areas off the Japanese mainland on 9 July 1945 in company with *Striker*. She transferred aircraft

to the fleet on 20 July and left for another load from Manus on 21 July. She arrived in Manus on 27 July, loaded up as quickly as possible and sailed again for the north on 29 July. Replacement aircraft were flown off on 6 August and she departed for Manus on 7 August. On 15 August she was ordered to return to Sydney where she was used briefly as a deck landing training (DLT) carrier for 899 Naval Air Squadron

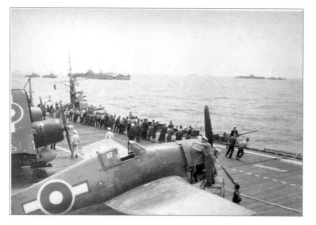

*Activity on **HMS Arbiter**'s flight deck during replenishment operations off Japan, probably on 20 July 1945. The Hellcat is having its engine panels replaced after last-minute work and other aircraft, including a Corsair IV are parked ready for transfer. Note the large number of ships in the replenishment area in the background. The sailors are hailing on a jackstay to transfer a pilot from a destroyer, just visible over the port deck edge.*

which was training RANVR (A) pilots, who had transferred from the RAAF, to fly Seafires.

After her brief spell as DLT carrier, *Arbiter* was ordered to Hong Kong where she embarked former Prisoners of War (POW) for repatriation to Australia.

She returned to Hong Kong on 3 December 1945 to embark another batch of former POWs, this time for repatriation to the UK. She returned to the Clyde to de-store in January 1946 and was returned to the USN at Norfolk Navy Yard in March 1946.

HMS Chaser *leaving Cochin with a ferry load of Corsair and Avenger aircraft.*

Chaser was allocated to the BPF in February 1945 after service with the Home Fleet during which she escorted convoys to North Russia. She arrived in Sydney in May 1945, loaded with replacement aircraft and sailed for the Air Train in Leyte Gulf. On 14 May she sailed from Leyte for the RAS areas off the Sakashima Islands and on 18 May, she transferred 3 Seafires, 2 Hellcats, 1 Firefly, 2 Avengers and 1 Corsair to 1 ACS. She recovered 3 Avenger and 1 Firefly "flyable duds". On 22 May she flew off another 10 aircraft with 4 more on 23 May before she set

heading to return to Manus.

She sailed from Manus for RAS operations off the mainland of Japan on 24 July 1945, transferring aircraft to the fleet on 31 July and 6 August. *Chaser* left the replenishment areas for Manus on 7 August and, with the end of hostilities, she proceeded to Sydney where she carried out a defect rectification period. On completion of the work package, she returned to the UK, de-stored and was returned to the USN at Norfolk Navy Yard on 12 May 1946.

HMS Ruler at sea in a replenishment area in May 1945. Note the crashed Avenger on the fo'c'sle.

HMS RULER

Ruler was allocated to the BPF in January 1945 after service with Western Approaches Command as a ferry carrier in the Atlantic. She was intended for use as a CAP carrier and worked up with the Hellcats of 885 NAS embarked before deploying. During her voyage to Australia, she also embarked the Fireflies of 1772 NAS for passage. She arrived in Sydney on 16 March 1945 and sailed for Leyte Gulf in April. She sailed from Leyte to cover RAS operations off the Sakashima Islands on 3 May 1945. By then 885 NAS had been expanded into a composite Hellcat/Avenger unit to provide both fighter CAP and anti-submarine protection for the BPF while it was in the replenishment areas. She covered RAS operations between 6 May and 18 May before returning to Leyte Gulf. After a brief stop in Leyte to refuel, she returned to Sydney, arriving on 5 June.

On 12 June 1945, *Ruler* sailed with 885 NAS embarked to cover RAS operations off the mainland of Japan in the BPF's third phase of operations. After the Japanese surrender, she entered Tokyo Bay with *Indefatigable* and other ships of the BPF on 31 August and was present for the surrender ceremony on USS *Missouri* on 2 September 1945. She sailed for Sydney on 13 September and left Sydney for the UK on 22 October. After de-storing in the Clyde in December, she was returned to the US Navy at Norfolk Navy Yard 29 January 1945.6 ?

HMS SLINGER

Slinger was allocated to the BPF in January 1945 after service as a ferry carrier in Western Approaches Command and a period as a DLT carrier. In February 1944 she had survived being mined in the approaches to Chatham Dockyard and spent from February to October 1944 in a London shipyard undergoing repairs. She arrived in Sydney on 22 February 1945 and sailed for Manus, with a load of aircraft, on 11 March. On 19 March she sailed from Manus for Leyte Gulf, arriving on 26 March. On 29 March she sailed for the RAS areas off the Sakashima Islands with a load of 25 replacement aircraft. She supplied 22 of them to the fleet on 5 April and recovered 2 "flyable duds". She returned to Leyte on 8 April and was in Sydney in July.

In August 1945, *Slinger* was used to repatriate former POWs from Hong Kong to Australia after which she carried out a defect rectification period in Sydney. She left Australia for the UK on 10 November and arrived in the Clyde to de-store in January 1946. She was returned to the USN at Norfolk Navy Yard in February 1946.

HMS SPEAKER

Speaker was allocated to the BPF as a CAP Carrier in January 1945 and arrived in Sydney on 23 February 1945 with the Hellcats of 1840 NAS embarked. While she was there, 1840 disembarked to RNAS Bankstown. It re-embarked on 9 March when *Speaker* sailed for the RAS areas off the Sakashima Islands after a brief stop at Manus. She flew CAP sorties over replenishment operations to give the fleet carriers' fighter squadrons a rest before joining the Air Train at Leyte Gulf on 23 April. While she was there, her role was changed from CAP carrier to replenishment carrier. Her Hellcats went into the "pool" of spare aircraft and the most experienced pilots, together with 70 maintenance ratings reinforced 5 Fighter Wing in *Indomitable*. The balance of pilots and maintainers went to *Ruler* where they could gain experi-

ence in the CAP role.

She had an eventful career as a replenishment carrier after sailing from Leyte on 4 May. During this period, 5 aircraft intended for *Indefatigable* had to be diverted during a period of radio silence. Aircraft handlers on the fleet carrier formed the word "*Speaker*" and the aircraft successfully got the message! Before leaving the fleet she embarked 20 wounded "cot cases" that resulted from Kamikaze attacks on *Victorious* and *Formidable*. They were transferred to the fleet hospital ship *Oxfordshire* in Leyte Gulf. *Speaker* sailed for a further period in the service areas on 19 May and transferred aircraft to the fleet on 23 May. She was back in Leyte on 29 May by which time 30 ACS had carried 190 aircraft to the service areas and transferred 140 of them to 1 ACS.

Speaker returned to Sydney in June to paint ship and to embark a load of aircraft and stores for RNAS Ponam. On 9 July she arrived at Ponam to disembark the aircraft and stores and take on board a replenishment load from the FAP. She sailed from Manus on 18 July and transferred aircraft to the fleet carriers on 26 July. *Striker* transferred 3 aircraft to her on 27 July and she transferred the balance of her aircraft to the fleet on 1 August before returning to Manus. On 13 August she sailed from Manus with a load of aircraft to replenish Task Group 38.5, the *Indefatigable* Group that remained in action when the remainder of the BPF withdrew to Australia to prepare for the proposed invasion of Japan, Operation "Olympic". 10 Seafires and a Firefly were flown off to *Indefatigable* on 20 August and 2 "flyable duds" were recovered. On completion of this evolution, *Speaker* was ordered to fly off all serviceable aircraft to *Ruler* and to make as much accommodation as possible available on board.

On 28 August Speaker was ordered to proceed to Tokyo Bay and on 29 August she was the first allied carrier to enter the Bay. *Ruler* followed her in on 31 August and took off all *Speaker's* air maintenance ratings to make more accommodation available. After the official surrender, she sailed for Manila with 477 Commonwealth former Prisoners of War on board. Captain "Jimmy" James took her to sea by a circuitous route over 12 miles that allowed every Commonwealth ship to cheer them. After landing them, she carried out two further repatriation runs, both of Americans from Nagasaki to Okinawa; the first group was of 899, the second of 645. At the same time USS *Chenango* carried survivors from HMS *Exeter* and HMAS *Perth* to the same destination. On 28 September *Speaker* arrived in Hong Kong and picked up Australian former POWs for passage to Sydney. More were picked up in Manila on route. She arrived in Sydney on 15 October 1945 and, whilst there, a diesel pipe burst and poured fuel into a diesel powered generator room. Repairs took some weeks but she was serviceable again by December. On 28 December she sailed with 721 NAS embarked. This was a Fleet Requirements Unit (FRU) equipped with Seafire and Vengeance aircraft which was to be re-deployed from RNAS Archerfield in Queensland to RNAS Kai Tak in Hong Kong. She arrived in Hong Kong on 10 January and, after unloading the FRU, sailed for a return trip to Sydney on 17 January via Manus. After a brief stop in Sydney she returned to the UK, arriving in the Clyde to de-store in June 1946. She was returned to the USN at Norfolk Navy Yard on 17 July 1946.

HMS VINDEX

Vindex was the only British-built escort carrier to serve with the BPF, the others all being American ships supplied to the RN under Lend/Lease arrangements. She had already had a long and distinguished career with Western Approaches Command and the Home Fleet when she was allocated to the BPF in May 1945. After conversion to the ferry role she sailed for Australia on 1 July with the Firefly night fighters of 1790 NAS embarked for passage. She anchored off Brisbane to unload aircraft and stores on 11 August and arrived in Sydney on 12 August 1945. With the Japanese surrender, plans to use her as a ferry carrier were shelved and she was loaded with 300 men and stores for the relief of Hong Kong. She sailed for

Brisbane and arrived there on 20 August to take on more stores, sailing on 23 August. After a brief stop at Manus, she arrived in Hong Kong on 8 September, hitting an unmarked wreck as she went alongside a berth in Kowloon. She embarked 300 Australian former POWs from the Stanley Internment Camp and sailed with them for Sydney on 18 September. She spent the remainder of 1945 ferrying passengers, stores and deck cargoes between Australia, Hong Kong and Iwakuni in Japan. On 30 November 1945

she collided with a junk in Hong Kong harbour adding to the damage incurred when she hit the wreck.

Vindex commenced a refit in the Garden Island Dockyard in Sydney on 9 February 1946 on completion of which she was used to transport the headquarters of the BPF from Sydney to Colombo. She arrived back in the UK on 23 September 1946 and, having been stripped of Admiralty equipment, she was sold back to the Port Line, her original owners before conversion from an escort carrier, for mercantile service.

HMS REAPER

Reaper was another late arrival in 30 ACS. She was allocated to the BPF in May 1945 after service in Western Approaches Command as a ferry carrier. Having been refitted in Rosyth Dockyard, she sailed for Australia on 23 July 1945 with a load of aircraft, arriving in Sydney on 13 September. She was at Manus on 3 October where she embarked the Sea Otters of RNAS Ponam's SAR Flight after which she

sailed for Hong Kong, arriving on 11 October. After a short stay, she returned to Sydney, arriving on 4 November. She visited Auckland in New Zealand on 17 November and then sailed for the UK, via Singapore on 19 November 1945. On 27 March 1946 she arrived in the Clyde to be de-stored before being returned to the USN at Norfolk Navy Yard on 20 May 1946.

HMS ACTIVITY

Activity arrived in Colombo to join the East Indies Fleet on 20 February 1945 and was lent to the BPF as a ferry carrier a day later. She carried a load of aircraft from Ceylon to Australia, leaving in late February.

She sailed from Sydney to return to Colombo on 24 March and, on arrival, returned to duties with the East Indies Fleet.

HMS BEGUM

Begum was allocated to the BPF for duty as a ferry carrier on 17 April 1945. She sailed from the Clyde on that date for Australia forming part of convoy KMF 43. She ferried the Vengeance aircraft of 721 NAS and the Sea Otters of 1701 NAS to Australia for fleet requirement duties based ashore and arrived in Sydney

to disembark them on 5 June 1945. On 15 June she sailed from Sydney for Manus with a load of aircraft for the FAP. After their delivery, she was re-allocated to the East Indies Fleet and sailed to Ceylon, arriving at Trincomalee on 2 July.

HMS FENCER

Fencer was allocated to the BPF after, extensive service with the Home Fleet, on 31 October 1944 for duty

as a ferry carrier. She arrived in Trincomalee on 22 November 1944 and was used to ferry aircraft

between Ceylon and Australia. On 31 March 1945 she sailed from Sydney for Leyte Gulf with a load of air-craft for the Air Train to pass on to the fleet carriers after which she left the BPF for a refit in Simonstown.

HOW REPLENISHMENT CARRIERS OPERATED

The replenishment carriers were the critical part of the whole operation. Without them the work of the MON-ABS, the TAMY, the Air Train, the FAP and the ferry carriers spread literally over the oceans of the world would have been of little use. The technique was per-fected during Operation "Iceberg" when the BPF operated off the Sakashima Islands. The following points are taken from the Report of Proceedings of that operation.

Before noon on the day before Replenishment at Sea (RAS) fleet carriers were instructed to signal ACS 1 with their requirements for replacement aircraft and aircrew. The ensuing total requirement was then sig-nalled to ACS 30 after the rendezvous in the service area by destroyer, message drop or visual signal as soon as possible. An abbreviated code was used in which aircraft types were indicated as follows:

ABLE	Hellcat
BAKER	Hellcat PR
EASY	Corsair II
FOX	Corsair IV
LOVE	Avenger II
PETER	Avenger I
QUEEN	Seafire LIII
ROGER	Seafire III
SUGAR	Firefly
TARE	Walrus
UNCLE	Sea Otter
ZEBRA	Flyable Duds

In using this code, the number of aircraft required placed in front of the code word for the type and the number of aircrew followed the word. An aircrew included pilot, observer and TAG where these were needed to operate the type of aircraft indicated. In multi-seat aircraft where the full crew was not required, a separate signal was to be sent.

For example if **Victorious** required 3 Avenger II with two full crews and 4 Corsair II without pilots and had an Avenger II "flyable dud" for disposal, she would have signalled:

To: AC 1
From: Victorious

3 LOVE 2. 4 EASY. ZEBRA 1 LOVE.

AC 1 staff would send a composite signal indicating each fleet carrier's replenishment requirements and the programme for transferring aircraft. AC 30 was to respond by informing AC 1 the name of the replenish-ment carrier to which each fleet carrier's ferry pilots should be sent and the name of the replenishment car-rier to which "flyable duds" were to be flown. AC 1 also had to be informed of the number of "flyable duds" that could be accepted on each replenishment carrier although in practice this was seldom a problem.

As soon as possible after rendezvous in the service area the fleet carriers would transfer ferry pilots to the replenishment carrier by aircraft or by jackstay trans-fer from a destroyer. They had to carry with them the requisite flying clothing, safety equipment including a parachute and anything else needed for the flight. Instructions called for replacement fighter aircraft to be delivered with empty drop tanks but a full outfit of ammunition. A note of the ammunition state was to be given to the ferry pilot when he accepted the aircraft.

SCR 522 radio sets were to be fitted with crystals for 116.1; 140.58 and 142.74 Megacycles and should be tuned to those frequencies. All crystals except 116.1 were to be removed from radio sets before despatch to a replenishment carrier. YE Beacon receivers were to be tuned to 575, 630, 660, 710, 760 and 785 Kilocycles and ferry pilots provided with the code in use before leaving their parent carriers. "Flyable duds" were to be transferred complete as far as was possible. Where, for urgent operational reasons, items of equipment were removed the reasons for doing so were to be recorded in the aircraft'' documentation. All aircraft were to be transferred with their log books and forms A 700.

Ideally, pilots who had flown "duds" to the replenishment carrier could fly replacement aircraft back to their own fleet carrier. If this was not practical, AC 30 was to signal AC 1 asking for transport.

The ideal loading for a replenishment carrier was 6 Avenger, 9 Corsair, 4 Seafire, 4 Hellcat and 1 Firefly, a total of 24 aircraft. It was not always possible, given fluctuations in the FAP to achieve this. Indeed given fluctuations in the losses suffered by the fleet carriers, it was not always desirable and flexibility was highly desirable. Given all the difficulties encountered in setting up the BPF's Air Train and the constant need for improvisation, the replenishment carriers and their supporting ferry carriers did extremely well.

Sources:

- Royal Navy Escort Carriers by David Hobbs. Published by Maritime Books in 2003
- Admiralty Pink Lists in the Archive of the Fleet Air Arm Museum.

Chapter Seven

THE MOBILE NAVAL AIRFIELD ORGANISATION

A MONAB Mobile Maintenance Component comprising an aircraft machine shop, two generator lorries, a battery charging lorry, general purpose workshop, electrical and instrument workshops.

The shore-based element of the naval air logistic organisation was the Mobile Naval Airfield Organisation (MNAO). It comprised two different types of unit, Mobile Operational Naval Air Bases (MONAB) and Transportable Aircraft Maintenance Yards (TAMY). The idea of the MONAB was probably conceived in 1942 based on the experience gained with naval air squadrons in the Norwegian campaign of 1940 and the North African campaign between 1941 and 1943. They had had no forward air bases of their own but a Mobile Air Torpedo Maintenance Unit had proved extremely useful. Whatever the origin, the concept was widely canvassed in naval staff papers during 1943, no doubt encouraged by the prospect of the Royal Navy's intended return to operations in the Pacific.

The original concept of the MONAB was "the rapid provision of facilities at airfields and airstrips for the training and maintenance of naval air squadrons disembarked from carriers operating in advance of existing bases". While not intended to provide for the operation of naval aircraft to operate from shore against the enemy, they were to provide, where necessary, key personnel and material peculiar to naval fly-

ing to enable naval aircraft to operate from airfields or advanced airstrips controlled by the RAF or any other Service. With the addition of small mobile maintenance, servicing or repair components, a MONAB could provide maintenance support for front-line aircraft and carry out small repairs quickly. Other MONABs were especially equipped to be capable of receiving, erecting, testing, maintaining and despatching the large number of replacement aircraft needed by the fleet to make good wastage during extended operations. Others still were capable accommodating and operating a Fleet Requirements Unit (FRU) or communications squadron in addition to disembarked front-line squadrons. Some MONABS, incorporating a suitable maintenance unit were intended to hold and service a pool of reserve, combat-ready aircraft at a forward base. In practice several of these functions were combined within individual MONABs in Australia.

No MONAB was expected to construct, maintain or defend its airfield or base, these duties being carried out, after agreement between the Admiralty and the War Office, by the Army. This was necessary because the Royal Navy had no equivalent to the US Navy's

A Mobile Air Radio Maintenance Unit which has radio and radar workshops housed in standard road/rail containers, normally mounted on 3-ton Bedford lorries. The two generator lorries are in the centre.

Mobile aircraft machine shop opened up to increase the available work space. The lowered flap was strong enough to be used as a work surface.

The interior of a Mobile Maintenance Unit battery charging lorry.

Construction Battalions, the famous CBs or "Seabees". These were made up of construction engineers from a civilian background whose boast, no idle one, was that "nothing is impossible". The nearest RN equivalents were the Royal Marines engineer units but these were rarely available in sufficient numbers. As a result of experience in the Pacific Theatre, the Admiralty strongly recommended the formation of a CB organisation within the Royal Navy but the war ended before it could be set up. The MONABs were equipped with no other weapons than hand-held sten-guns and pistols.

The personnel complements required by MONABs depended on the function they were intended to perform but each was to be entirely self-sufficient. This meant that men had to be provided to fulfil a wide variety of tasks which included air traffic control, cooking, baking, medical support and the maintenance of motor transport, boats, cranes, tents and mobile hangars. By July 1945, complements of 2,000 and more were common.

The second component of the MNAO was the TAMY. This was equipped with a full range of work-shops, aircraft stores and equipment capable of undertaking major repairs and overhauls to airframes, engines and components. It was also capable of reducing to produce aircraft that were beyond economic repair. In composition and organisation the TAMY was necessarily more complex and less mobile than a MONAB and was expected to need a longer period to reach maturity. The TAMY was expected to be located near the fleet's main base and not in the forward area. Its personnel had to be more skilled in maintenance than those in the MONABs. In addition

Lister generator lorry with its canopy removed for the photographer. The canopy was normally left on when the generator was running.

" Something to do with this new MONAB business, I think."

Something of the way the MONABs were perceived at the time can be imagined from this cartoon taken from the January 1945 edition of "Flight Deck", the Fleet Air Arm's in-house journal.

A Mobile Servicing Component Workshop (above) and the interior of a Radar Workshop (below).

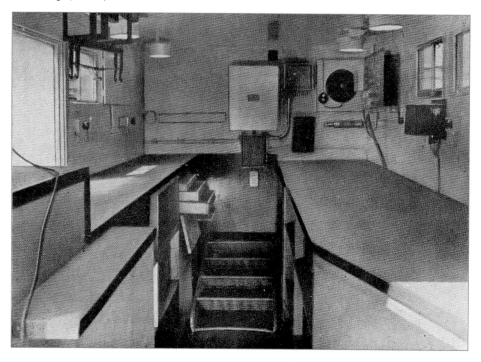

A General Purpose Workshop (above) and the interior of an Aircraft Machine Shop (below).

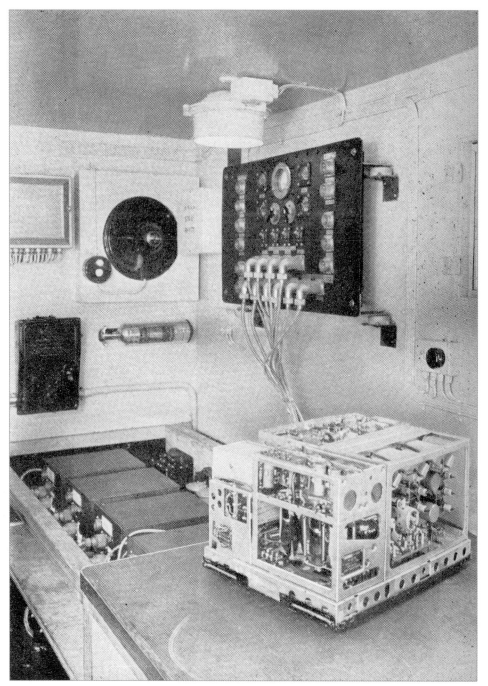

Inside a mobile radar workshop.

to the components that one might have found in a MONAB, the TAMY had specialist sections that covered the provision of facilities. These included buildings or portable hangars, equipment and personnel for technical offices and administration, large aircraft workshops, engine overhaul and repairs, ancillary workshops, propeller repairs, dope and paint shops and workshops for breaking down aircraft to spares and produce. Armament, radio and radar repairs were included in the range of tasks that could be undertaken. In early 1944 it was decided to form five MONABs and one TAMY in the UK intended for service in the Far East. RAF Ludham in Norfolk was taken over for the purpose and commissioned as a naval air station, *HMS Flycatcher*. MONABs assembled there at the rate of one a month until the end of 1944 when Ludham was handed back to the RAF and *Flycatcher* moved to Middle Wallop in Wiltshire which was, in turn, commissioned as a naval air station. By then, Admiralty plans included eleven MONABs and two

TAMYs with the possibility that the former figure would rise to fifteen by 1946. By VJ Day, however, only nine MONABs and one TAMY had left the UK with a tenth forming at Middle Wallop. Six of these, and the TAMY took over air stations or establishments, some of them only half built, in Australia. They were vacated by the Royal Australian Air Force, the US Navy and Marine Corps and civilian firms.

In detail, a MONAB comprised a number of specialised components. These included command and secretariat, a fully equipped sick bay, stores accounting and domestic services such as cooking and baking. From an aircraft support viewpoint, the MONAB could include some or all of the following components:

Mobile Servicing Component (MS) - consisted of four lorries. Of these, one was equipped as a workshop; two as universal stores carriers and one as a general-purpose vehicle to carry ground equipment. The com-

The early stage of erecting a Dorland Hangar.

ponent was expected to support the servicing of 25 aircraft for 14 days but did not include the maintenance personnel.

Mobile Maintenance Component (MM) - comprised six specialist lorries. One machine shop, one electrical and instrument workshop, one general-purpose workshop, one battery charging and two generator lorries made up a self-contained mobile workshop unit. Ground and servicing equipment and a wide range of spares were intended to make the component, accompanied by the necessary personnel, capable of servicing 50 aircraft for one month. This component was also intended to enable minor inspections and the repair by replacement of complete assemblies. Two Dorland hangars were provided for this work to be carried out under cover.

Mobile Servicing and Maintenance (MSM) Pack Up - included all the equipment found in one MM and two MS components but took the form of a crated pack-up for installation in airfield buildings rather than lorries. The component was intended for use in MONABs near the main fleet base that were expected to be static.

Mobile Personnel Component (MP) - consisted of maintenance personnel with their own tool kits and was expected to support a single squadron that had disembarked without its maintenance ratings.

Mobile Storage and Reserve Component (MSR) - capable of being added to any MONAB and, with the necessary personnel and ground equipment, was intended to maintain 50 aircraft in storage. A Dorland hangar was provided for maintenance work.

Mobile Repair Component (MR) Pack Up - a large range of machine tools and equipment which, when added to a MONAB, enabled it to carry out major inspections. The MR was intended for use in the main base area, especially if MS and MM components had moved to advanced bases. Two Brook hangars were provided offering sufficient gantry space for sixteen concurrent aircraft engine changes.

Mobile Air Radio Maintenance Component (MAR) - comprised three radio and four radar workshops, two stores and two 22 kW lorries of the same basic type as those used by the MM component. The workshops

A Dorland Hangar nearing completion, showing both the framework and the canvas cover.

By 1944 the Royal Navy employed a vast airfield construction organisation, worldwide. This is a naval air station under construction in Ceylon.

and stores were mounted in standard road/rail containers normally mounted on 3 ton Bedford chassis.

In addition to these, there were a number of other, smaller, components such as Naval Air Radio Repair (NARR). Special Maintenance Parties (SMP), introduced two years earlier in the UK for work on individual types of aircraft, were also employed both in Australia and in the forward area at Manus.

As the MONABs' planned essential feature was mobility they relied on a large number of specialist and general-purpose vehicles to achieve the aim. These included 31 specialist lorries, 55 non-specialist lorries,

34 trailers, 36 special road/rail containers for stores and spares and a dozen or more jeeps. The specialist lorries included wireless transmitting vehicles, radar beacon vans, photographic workshops, aircraft control vans, generators and camp lighting lorries. There were also breakdown vehicles, crash tenders, cranes, bowsers and fuel tankers, a water purification plant lorry and water trailers. Lorries fulfilled functions as offices, laundries, bakeries and NAAFI shops. Sick Bays operated from mobile dispensaries. Even from this short list it will be seen that the maintenance of the vehicles was nearly as big a problem as that of the aircraft. The problem was compounded in many cases by the inad-

equate servicing given to the vehicles in the UK and their lack of preservation during the long sea voyage to Australia. Many were loaded in the rain in Liverpool in the UK winter and found to be badly corroded when they were unloaded onto the docks in Sydney.

Motor Transport (MT) was the responsibility of Royal Marines Motor Transport Detachments, one of which was attached to each MONAB or TAMY. Most were seriously under strength when they arrived in Australia and had little on no training in vehicle maintenance. Of interest, the majority of RM Officers-in-Charge of MT had not even been taught to drive when they arrived in Australia. No MT maintenance equipment or even hand tools had been provided and this, coupled with the inexperience of the mechanics caused a major problem. Had the MONABs gone directly to a Pacific Island near the combat area, these deficiencies could well have been critical. The problem was resolved however by miss-employing aircraft mechanics, using local contractors in the Sydney and Brisbane areas and with considerable help from RAAF transport units.

Once vehicles got onto the Australian roads, they suffered a high accident rate. About twelve vehicles per month were damaged beyond local repair mainly, it was believed, due to the inexperience of the drivers. These added to the overall maintenance problems and a recommendation was made that all future MONABs should have mobile MT workshops supported by a thoroughly trained staff. These should be supported by an efficient administrative office capable of planning the employment and keeping maintenance records for all vehicles.

THE TRANSFER AND CONSTRUCTION OF AIRFIELDS FOR THE ROYAL NAVY IN AUSTRALIA

Four RAAF airfields were selected for transfer to the RN in November 1944 and a works programme agreed upon to modify them for naval requirements. Nowra, roughly 80 miles south of Sydney was intended to act as a base for up to 90 aircraft. In addition to the MONAB, it was to have a Mobile Aircraft Torpedo Maintenance Unit (MATMU). It was hoped to have the airfield ready by December 1944 but it was actually taken over from January 1945. Jervis Bay, about 20 miles east of Nowra, was also to be capable of taking 90 aircraft, with both a MONAB and a MATMU. It was hoped to have it ready by March 1945 but it was not taken over until 28 April. Schofields, roughly 30 miles west of Sydney, was originally intended to support fighter squadrons. It was taken over on schedule in February 1945 but in a very incomplete state. The last of the original four was Bankstown, 12 miles south west of Sydney. This was required as a Receipt and Despatch Unit capable of erecting 70 aircraft from delivery by sea at first, rising to 200 per month. It was also intended to store up to 500 reserve aircraft for the BPF. It was occupied in January 1945, some weeks earlier than the original plan. Considerable works were set in train at all these locations but none were completely finished when the war ended, unexpectedly, on 15 August. Plans for the MNAO had been long term and had been intended to provide support for the 1st, 11th and 30th Aircraft Carrier Squadrons through 1946, and possibly into 1947.

By May 1945 the staff of VA (Q) and FONAP were aware that the works programmes were taking very much longer than had been expected. They sought to alleviate the problem by obtaining additional air stations that would need fewer alterations than those already selected. If a sufficient number of more fully built up airfields could not be obtained from the RAAF, then one or two of those required in 1946 might have to be developed around existing airstrips, although this idea was deprecated as it had the potential to create even more work. Most of the RAAF airfields in question had been built hastily in the early months of the Pacific War in 1942. By 1945 they were breaking up and incapable of the sort of concentrated use that the BPF wished to make of them. The following airfield sites were proposed by the RN to meet its growing needs:

A Bakery Trailer, one of the many specialised vehicles which deployed with a MONAB. These units were capable of baking 144 2lb loaves every 70 minutes.

Evans Head   Required by August 1945
Narromine   Required by September 1945
Greenhills   Required by October 1945
Coffs Harbour   Required by November 1945
Cecil Plains   Required by December 1945
Leyburn   Required by January 1946

These dates were wildly optimistic but served as the basis for negotiation. After further discussion with the Australian authorities, Greenhills and Coffs Harbour were selected for closer scrutiny. Both comprised nothing but basic airstrips with no buildings at the latter but layout plans were prepared for both. In the event, the war ended before anything further could be

achieved at these sites but the Australian Government's reallocation of labour and materials towards housing projects meant that little would have been achieved during 1945.

On 8 July 1945 VA (Q) was concerned that this reduction in labour and materials would probably reduce work on naval air stations to the resurfacing of the runways at Maryborough, completing Evans Head by the end of August and completing Narromine by the end of October. A small number of Royal Marines Engineer Units (RMEU) had become available to help with these tasks. Work on Coffs Harbour was to commence when these projects were completed, hopefully by December 1945. The Australian Government

officials always quoted for manpower in terms of money and by the end of July, detailed investigations showed that there was sufficient to start work on Evans Head, Maryborough and, if drastic cuts were made in the works schedules for all air stations, on Narromine as well. A meeting was held on 23 July to formalise this view and substantial cuts were made to the proposed schedules for Maryborough, Evans Head, Bankstown, Jervis Bay and TAMY 1.

A further meeting was held in Melbourne on 28 July. At this the RAAF agreed to transfer Parkes to the RN in mid-December 1945 and West Sale, near Melbourne, in January 1946. A reconnaissance party was to evaluate Oakey and Amberley to decide which was the more suitable to take MONAB 8 with Amberley eventually being decided upon. The meeting also decided to initiate a detailed examination of what could be removed from the works packages at

Narromine and Coffs Harbour and to determine whether the latter could be developed by an RMEU, thus salvaging work on another site in 1946.

RMEUs were actually sent to Maryborough, Evans Head and Coffs Harbour to commence the work schedules but the war ended before very much could be done by them. The end of the war caused a complete change of programme. Amberley, Narromine, Evans Head, Parkes and West Sale were all cancelled. Further, Australian labour was withdrawn and works at the other air stations that were less than 80% complete had to be cancelled.

In hindsight it is clear that planners in the UK over-estimated the need for mobility. Nor had they foreseen the extent to which the early MONABs were mainly a convenient way of establishing "permanent" naval air stations in the main base. Had the early MONABs been deployed to a site without the sophisticated sup-

A mobile workshop for the maintenance of airborne radar.

port found in Australia they would have encountered grave difficulty in operating but they were not. Given their limitations, they achieved outstanding results and produced results without which the Air Train could not have supported the BPF in action for much of 1945. The most important lesson was that MONABs did have a very important role to play in modern war. However, they relied on outside agencies such as the USN Construction Battalions in the forward area and civilian construction firms in the main base to create the airfields they were to move into. MONABs also relied on the industrial base they found in Australia for many things beside construction. These included engineering in its broadest sense, transport, local purchase and stores to fill the many gaps in their planned outfits. Despite a very strong recommendation form the C-in-C BPF that the RMEUs should be expanded into something like the SeaBees, the Admiralty failed to take the idea forward in the constrained post-war era. The Royal Navy lost a potential capability that would have been both valuable and widely used. The British Army and RAF had both failed to provide the capability under wartime conditions but were both quick to reclaim the role as theirs in peacetime after 1945.

MONAB 2 sources:

- Report on the Organisation of the Flag Officer Naval Air Pacific in the Archive of the Fleet Air Arm Museum.
- Fleet Air Arm magazine Flight Deck, January 1945.
- Engineering in the Royal Navy, reprinted from the British Machine Tool Engineering Journal in June 1945.
- The Forgotten Bases by J D Brown. Part of The History of the Royal Australian Navy in World War II Second Edition, edited by David Stevens. Published by Allen and Unwin, Crow's Nest NSW in 2005.

Chapter Eight

MONAB 1

HMS Nabbington
RNAS Nowra
RNAS Jervis Bay

RNAS Nowra 1945.

The first MONAB began to form at RNAS Ludham on 4 September 1944 under Commander G Nunnerley RN. It was a self-accounting unit with its own executive, administrative, stores, medical and catering elements in addition to the aircraft engineering and air traffic control teams. All MONABs were to be given ships' names beginning with the letters "Nab" and number 1 commissioned as HMS *Nabbington* on 28 October 1944. RNAS Ludham itself was a disused RAF airfield that had only been taken over by the Admiralty on 24 August and commissioned on 4 September as HMS

Flycatcher. Its ship's company was far from ready to train operational MONABs and in consequence many sailors had to help with communal establishment duties rather than learn their new roles when they arrived on draft. To make matters worse many officers and ratings only arrived a few days prior to embarkation and were given very little training. Some of the new arrivals were found to be too old or medically unfit for overseas service, especially for the expeditionary role originally intended for the unit. Had they been ordered to proceed to a forward airstrip on a Pacific Island as originally intended they would have

had no idea about elementary tropical hygiene and could hardly have functioned. For their time at Ludham, there was little transport; no training area set out for personnel to practice setting up a mobile airfield and no lecture rooms or cinemas to show instructional films. Such training as there was comprised practical instruction in the use of small arms such as the Sten gun and combat skills since it was believed that MONAB personnel would have to follow close behind assault landings on remote islands before setting up their base. Reality was to prove somewhat different.

The most important factor during the form-up period, however, was time. The Admiralty saw the deployment of the first MONAB to the British Pacific Fleet's main base in Australia as imperative if the recently formed fleet was to be sustained in action. Most vehicles arrived at Ludham before MONAB 1 embarked but the radio and radar vans had to be shipped later with MONAB 2's stores. Much of their time was spent queuing to draw battle dress, webbing and small arms, as they became available. Interestingly, officers and men were required to carry their more formal blue and white uniforms with them wherever they went in case they were re-appointed or drafted. This could prove inconvenient while they lived in tents!

MONAB 1 was intended initially to provide support for a variety of squadrons operating Avenger, Corsair, Hellcat and Martlet aircraft. This was to be achieved by providing maintenance at all levels and the control of flying operations from a large airfield to give continuation and refresher flying. Among the components that made up the mobile base were MM 1, MS 1 and MS 2, MSR 1 and a MATMU. 723 NAS, which formed separately at Townhill Camp in Fifeshire, was intended to operate from the base when it was established. If necessary, this support was to be provided from an island base relatively close to the replenishment areas, once the BPF moved away from its main base in Australia.

On completion of its time at Ludham, the personnel embarked in the troopship SS *Empress of Scotland* at Liverpool on 20 November 1944. The vehicles were driven to Birkenhead where they joined the crated stores and were loaded into SS *Suffolk* for passage.

Both ships sailed to Australia through the Panama Canal and across the Pacific, a journey that took about a month.

In common with all the MONABS, Number 1 had insufficient time to open the stores and catalogue them. Most were supplied with SNSO, dockyard or manufacturers' identification codes which bore no resemblance to the aircraft part numbers that would be demanded by squadrons, carriers and the air element of the Fleet Train in Australia. Many of the stores ratings were unfamiliar with air stores and had time only to re-label crates for the relevant docks when they arrived at Ludham. Even the handling of stores at Ludham had its problems as the majority arrived by rail and the station was a small country halt. Many vehicles had to meet goods wagons, drive crates to RNAS Ludham where they were re-labelled and taken back to the station to be re-loaded into another wagon. The vehicles' journey to the docks took several days with inexperienced drivers moving as a slow convoy through roads congested with other military traffic. Road signs had been removed for the duration and maps were not always reliable. A number of vehicles had minor accidents in the blackout. Once at the docks the vehicles were not cleaned or given preservative treatment but loaded complete with mud and rainwater as they were. These comments, taken from the unit's Report of Proceedings (ROP), highlight some of the MONABs' shortcomings. It was, however, a considerable achievement to have assembled the unit and transported it with most of its specialist vehicles against the background of manpower and equipment shortages in Britain in the fifth year of a global war. The production of MONABs at monthly intervals that were capable of providing support for disembarked BPF squadrons within days of their arrival at an unfamiliar airfield, 12,000 miles from the UK, was one of the great achievements of the Royal Navy in World War 2.

Several of MONAB 1's senior officers were flown to Australia with the intention that they were to make arrangements for the full unit when it arrived. Their transport arrangements were much delayed, however, and they only arrived 24 hours before the *Empress of Scotland*, which arrived in Sydney on 18 December

1944. The unit was, by then, no longer expected to occupy a forward base but was, instead, to take over an RAAF airfield at Nowra in New South Wales, about 80 miles south of Sydney and not far from the fleet exercise areas in Jervis Bay. In view of MONAB 1's lack of training and equipment this had to be considered fortunate. At first the personnel moved into tented accommodation at Warwick Farm Racecourse, part of HMS *Golden Hind*, the RN Barracks in Sydney. The ship carrying stores, vehicles and equipment arrived in Sydney docks on Christmas Eve and unloading commenced immediately. The RN had nothing with which to undertake this task[1] so it was carried out to a large extent by the RAAF's Number 1 Transport and Movement Office (TMO). The RAAF not only helped to unload the ship but also serviced the vehicles, which were in poor state after the voyage, to the best of its ability. RAAF vehicles were used to transport stores to Nowra but the majority of personnel had travelled by train, arriving from 21 December.

Without this help, the air station could probably not have opened until late January and thus might not have been functional before the BPF arrived in Sydney. With the help, it was able to take over administrative control of the airfield and hoist the white ensign as HMS *Nabbington*, RNAS Nowra, on 2 January 1945.

Flying control and meteorological services were handed over to the RN in mid January when the last of the RAAF officers departed. With the commissioning of the air station, the unit effectively ceased to be mobile and set about carrying out the duties that would have been expected of a large air station in the UK, albeit with less manpower. The technical vans and workshops were still of value, however, as the permanent installations were far from complete. The MATMU was set up in its own compound off the Princes Highway, the main access to the airfield. It was established to support the US 22-inch torpedoes used by Avenger aircraft but these saw no operational use in the BPF. Whilst the mobile workshops proved immediately useful, the mobile communications and radar facilities proved rather more difficult to set up. Fred Fellowes has recorded his memories of arriving at Nowra from Warwick Farm on Christmas Day 1944 with the radar installation group. The team set up their

trailers on Nowra Hill and got them working but results were not good enough. After several days they moved the whole unit to Greenwell Point but again found disappointing results. They eventually moved to Kinghorn Head, Wheelers Point where satisfactory results where obtained.

One of the first officers to arrive was Lieutenant (A) Hugh Langrishe RNVR. After the war he spoke of helping RAAF officers to serve Christmas dinner in the Airmen's Mess during the period of the handover. He also recalled that the runways caused problems. They had been constructed in 1942 of a sealed layer of gravel and sand, compacted by sheep's feet and rollers. On top of this was 1-inch of rolled, tarred gravel. The resulting surface had worked adequately for three years' use by Marauder and Beaufort bombers but the touchdown points rapidly broke up after the arrival of naval aircraft. This was probably due to the severe impact loading caused by carrier-style landings, aggravated by the small wheel area in contact with the ground and the heavy use to which the runways were put in early 1945. Their condition was made worse by inefficient drainage and a particularly wet spell in April 1945[2]. In the short term the problem was solved by moving the touchdown points, there being sufficient runway length to do so safely but, eventually, the runways had to be taken out of use on 7 March and reconstruction work was carried out until 27 April. During this period the airfield at Jervis Bay was used and manned by MONAB 1. The problem does not seem to have arisen at other naval air stations in Australia although the runway construction method cannot have been unique.

The haste with which MONAB 1 deployed to Australia was justified. The fleet carriers arrived in Australian waters in early February after Operation Meridian, the strikes on the Sumatran oil refineries. They needed to replace their aircraft losses, which amounted to about a quarter of their embarked complement, and to provide shore-based continuation flying for the aircrew while the carriers were alongside in Sydney preparing for the next series of operations. Squadrons disembarked on 9 and 10 February 1945 as the ships of the 1st Aircraft carrier Squadron arrived off Jervis Bay. Nominally six aircraft from each

squadron were flown ashore to Nowra, a total of about sixty aircraft from ten squadrons. These comprised 1839 and 1844 Hellcat squadrons from *Indomitable*, 1830, 1833, 1834 and 1836 Corsair squadrons from *Illustrious* and *Victorious* and the Avengers of 849, 854, 857 and 820 squadrons. The latter disembarked from *Victorious*, *Illustrious*, *Indomitable* and *Indefatigable*. The numbers had to be limited to about a quarter of the embarked aircraft because parking areas were barely adequate even for that number and aircraft had to be parked on the grass beside the runways. Also greater numbers of aircrew would have overwhelmed wardroom messing facilities. By using the carriers for accommodation, it proved possible to rotate aircrew between Sydney and Nowra, allowing some continuation flying and a short leave period. Replacement aircraft were taken on charge from MONAB 2 at Bankstown, which had done a remarkable job to assemble sufficient to bring the squadrons up to operational strength.

849 Naval Air Squadron's disembarkation from *Victorious* gives some idea of the early days of MONAB 1's operations. A number of squadrons were launched from the fleet with instructions to make landfall at Cape Howe, then fly up the coast to Jervis Bay, from where, the briefing officer claimed, they could see the airfield at Nowra. Lieutenant (A) "Chick" Chandler RNVR subsequently recorded that the fighters, with their faster transit speed, did just that but as

849's Avengers neared Jervis Bay, the weather deteriorated with low cloud and poor visibility. They were led by the Senior Pilot, Lieutenant (A) Donald Judd, whose observer, as group navigator, had the only navigational aid, an 8 by 5 inch map of Australia on which Nowra was shown as an ink dot! Repeated radio requests for the base weather report and a course to steer that was clear of high ground over the unfamiliar country only got the reply "Roger". Eventually, air traffic control at Nowra advised them that a road from the southern end of Jervis Bay would lead them to the base. The first attempt was made in "vee" formation at 200 feet flying along the road but they lost sight of it among trees. After turning back to Jervis Bay they found a "T" junction (which still exists and serves as a land mark for aviators) and followed the road to the north west encouraged by Nowra's advice that the Avenger's engines could be heard. Most of the aircraft had flown past the airfield when the extreme port wing aircraft waggled his wings and turned hard to port, followed by the rest of the squadron. The last aircraft landed on before the first had cleared the runway.

The squadrons from *Indomitable*, *Victorious* and *Indefatigable* re-embarked on 27 and 28 February. *Illustrious* was suffering from vibration problems and had been docked in the Captain Cook dry dock in Garden Island Dockyard at Sydney for the removal of her centre screw. Her three squadrons did not re-embark until 7 March by which time the other carriers

Parade of MONAB personnel through Nowra on what was known at that time as VP Day, now known as VJ Day - 15 August 1945.

(Courtesy of Tony Drury)

were working up off Manus in preparation for Operation Iceberg.

The departure of the front line squadrons left capacity for the build up of a number of second line units. 723 Naval Air Squadron had sailed for Australia in December 1944. Personnel arrived at Nowra on 27 January 1945 under the command of Lieutenant Commander H A P Bullivant RNR and began to operate a daily service to Mascot airfield in Sydney with Expeditor aircraft. This task was taken over by 724 NAS, based at Bankstown, in April 1945. After the runway problems at Nowra, the squadron made use of the runway at Jervis Bay as it expanded to its establishment of eight Martinets, eight Corsairs and two Expeditors. A number of Hellcats were added later in 1945. On 28 February, 723 officially formed at RNAS Bankstown as a Fleet Requirements Unit to support warships working up in Jervis Bay. Since Bankstown only had a grass runway, however, the aircraft mainly made use of Nowra or Jervis Bay. The Martinets towed "sleeve" targets at the end of a long wire for the fleet to shoot at but the fighters carried out "throw off" shoots. In these, the aircraft dived at ships which opened fire on them with live ammunition but with their guns offset 15 degrees to port of the bearing indicated by the ships' sights, an exciting experience for the pilots many of whom had only recently completed training. 723 moved from Bankstown to Jervis Bay while the runways at Nowra were being repaired and

to Nowra itself on 4 June. It moved again to RNAS Schofields in January 1946.

706 Naval Air Squadron was established as a second line unit to keep replacement aircrew in flying practice and to carry out conversion training. Its aircrew left the UK on 2 February 1945 and assembled at Jervis Bay under Lieutenant Commander (A) R E Bradshaw DSC* RN. First equipment comprised two Corsairs and two Avengers with maintenance ratings "borrowed" from MONAB 1. The unit expanded rapidly with representative aircraft of all the six types to be used by the BPF. It moved to Schofields in March, taking with it the Corsair and Avenger MSRs from MONAB 1, as they were no longer required at Nowra.

In addition to providing facilities for disembarked squadrons, Nowra administered range facilities at Currarong. These were also used by aircraft from other air stations in the Sydney area and proved a most valuable asset in keeping squadron pilots' combat skills at an acceptable level. As the training pipeline expanded, they were of importance to bring new and inexperienced pilots and armourers up to the standard required. A shortage of explosive stores such as rocket projectiles and cannon ammunition was the only constraint on armament training. Sufficient supplies only became available in August when the war ended.

Captain H G Dickinson RN moved from MONAB 5 to relieve Commander Nunnerley as Commanding Officer on 9 March 1945. In his Report of

Proceedings (ROP) he stressed the positive achievements of the unit but pointed out the many shortcomings in the MONAB's training and equipment. To be fair, he did comment that the general lack of engineering equipment was due more to the unit's employment administering a large naval air station and not the temporary airstrip in a forward operating area it was created to run. This was a much greater task than had been intended for such an organisation and its equipment by the planners. Like many other COs he commented on lack of stores and spare parts but this was a problem facing the entire Royal Navy as it struggled to come to terms with the importance of logistic support in the new form of warfare it was committed to fighting.

Once the runways were repaired, Nowra began to see more activity supporting disembarked front line squadrons and working up the planned spare or replacement air groups. Number 3 CAG was the first of these and 854 NAS was allocated to it when it disembarked from *Illustrious*. By June, when the fleet carriers returned for their replenishment period in Sydney there were five disembarked squadrons. These were 1839 and 1844 with Hellcats and 857 with Avengers from *Indomitable* which was in refit in Sydney plus 849 with Avengers from *Victorious* and 854. When the war ended in August there were nine, 1839, 1844 with Hellcats; 1841, 1842 and 1846 with

Corsairs and 828, 848, 854 and 857 with Avengers. With the post war demobilisation of the BPF, some of these units became "paper" squadrons with few personnel and no flying. The need to support the carriers that were to remain with the fleet, however, meant that a sizeable flying task continued into the autumn as their air groups disembarked while the ships were in Australian waters.

In September the Fireflies of 1771 NAS disembarked from *Implacable* and remained there until they disbanded on 16 October. *Indomitable's* two Hellcat squadrons disembarked on 11 October and disbanded leaving the aircraft at Nowra while the personnel sailed home with their ship. On 24 October 3 CAG was disbanded and its aircraft left to be ditched at sea. 837 NAS moved to Nowra from Jervis Bay on 29 October to exchange its Barracudas for Fireflies.

MONAB 1, HMS *Nabbington* had been the first unit of its kind to form and was in consequence the first to be returned to the UK after the end of hostilities. It was paid off on 15 November 1945 so that its personnel could be re-appointed, re-drafted or released. It was replaced at Nowra by MONAB 5 from Jervis Bay, which retained its commissioned name as HMS *Nabswick*. It continued to run Nowra as a "permanent" air station with a flying task that was to continue into 1946.

MONAB 1 sources:

- Report on the Organisation of the Flag Officer Naval Air Pacific in the Archive of the Fleet Air Arm Museum.
- The Development of British Naval Aviation Volume III – unpublished Naval Staff History in the Author's possession.
- Report of the Experience of the British Pacific Fleet – 1946 in the Archive of the Fleet Air Arm Museum.
- *HMAS Albatross* - A Collection of Memories by Mike Lehan. Published by the Australian Naval Aviation Museum in 2000.
- The Squadrons of the Fleet Air Arm by Ray Sturtivant & Theo Balance. Published by Air Britain in 1994.
- *www.faahistoryweb*

Chapter Nine

MONAB 2

HMS Nabberley
RNAS Bankstown

RNAS Bankstown under construction in 1945. Note the number of aircraft on the hardstanding at the top of the picture.

The second MONAB began to form at RNAS Ludham in October 1944, under the command of Commander E P F Atkinson RN. The formation of the first unit had been difficult but the second became more so because of an early decision to change its role. The first ratings had already joined when it was decided to transform it from an operating base into a mobile Receipt and Despatch Unit (RDU), responsible for erecting, modifying and storing naval aircraft as they arrived in the Pacific Theatre. No scheme of complement existed for such a unit and it was difficult to envisage what would be required of it

when it deployed. The Fleet Air Arm Drafting Office at RNAS Lee-on-Solent was not informed of the change in time and had already started the drafting process for a 'normal' MONAB. The Principal Medical Officer (PMO) believed that few drafting offices actually knew what a MONAB was because of the number of ratings who arrived at Ludham with documents marked "Unfit for service overseas"! MONAB 2 eventually formed with the normal headquarters, supply and medical components but there were no MM or MS components. Instead there were an Aircraft Erection Unit, Aircraft Equipment and

Modification Unit and an Aircraft Storage Unit.

A complement of 997 technical ratings was finally decided upon. Ludham could not accommodate that number and, as a further complication, the ratings initially drafted for MONAB 2 were not used and a further 997 were drafted to meet the requirement. 600 of these had to be accommodated at HMS *Gosling*, a technical training establishment for air fitters and mechanics, at Risley near Warrington, that was used, among other things, to give aerodrome defence training to Royal Marines. The split made kitting up and the management of short courses at the Schools of Aircraft Maintenance (SAM) more difficult than they would otherwise have been.

As a consequence of their short notice drafts, the newly arrived ratings were largely unfamiliar with the types of aircraft on which they were expected to work. Since the date of sailing was fixed and unchangeable, there was little opportunity to arrange suitable courses and it had to be accepted that technical ratings would familiarise themselves with aircraft "on the job". No ratings trained in the cataloguing and checking of air stores were included in the initial scheme of complement and nor were there any writers in the workshop complement. When three were provided at the last possible moment, only one could type. Despite all the difficulties, MONAB 2 was commissioned as HMS *Nabberley* at Ludham on 11 November 1944.

The unit's vehicles and equipment moved to join the stores in a compound at the Gladstone Dock in Liverpool on 20 November 1944. They were embarked in SS *Perthshire* and sailed for Australia a day later. The personnel embarked in SS *Athlone Castle* in Liverpool during December and sailed for Australia on 22 December. Both ships passed through the Panama Canal and crossed the Pacific.

The unit arrived in Sydney on 26 January 1945 and began to move into Bankstown 12 miles to the southwest. The site was formally taken over from the RAAF three days later on 29 January, on which day it commissioned formally as HMS *Nabberley*, RNAS Bankstown. From the outset it became obvious that what was required was not a mobile unit but a permanent RDU, very like those established in the UK and Mediterranean theatres. Eight Corsairs and eight

Martinets had already arrived from RNAY Cochin in southern India and a working party from HMS *Unicorn* had helped with the work of preparing them for squadron use. The RAAF had transported aircraft from Sydney both in crates and standing on their wheels and had gamely helped with the work of erecting them. They were not used to the naval aircraft types, however and progress was slow. Naval personnel gradually took over the erection process fully and, as the sailors grew familiar with the work, the RAAF withdrew leaving only a few key senior airmen by the end of February. A works programme was set in train to enlarge the existing facilities but was not completed by the end of the war.

A number of factors slowed the new RDU's progress toward erecting the number of aircraft projected for it, the most obvious being the inexperienced manpower. The lack of sufficient cranes and jacks slowed production, as aircraft often had to wait for a crane to be free before certain components could be fitted. There was a lack of publications and forms and the ROP mentions references to new instructions that were not available in Australia, let alone Bankstown! Because the airfield was a grass strip, weather often influenced the ability to carry out test flights with newly assembled aircraft. Wet weather led to a muddy surface and sunny weather led to dust clouds and pitting. Another factor that was learnt in the first weeks was the need for close liaison with FONAP Headquarters in Sydney over the allotment of airframes to replenishment carriers and squadrons. It was found more practical for the staff in Sydney to state the type and number of aircraft to be issued and to leave the selection of individual airframes to the RDU. The alternative method was too open to misunderstanding and error. Lastly, the practice of ferrying aircraft with secret equipment removed caused considerable delay in trying to trace the two elements and bring them together for issue. When dealing with large numbers of airframes, it was found much better to deal with ones that had all their equipment within them, especially when they had been made airtight by being coated in Erenol. It was found that American aircraft that were so treated, even those that had travelled as deck cargo, could be rapidly depreserved and

none showed any trace of corrosion.

Aircraft were received in various states of installation, some arriving completely installed, others partly installed and, in many cases, devoid of all equipment, it having been despatched separately. In the majority of cases, the equipment fitted in aircraft was in perfect condition. Equipment in partially complete aircraft caused considerable delays, as spare components had to be found for them. Equipment sent separately was often found to be damaged due to bad packing and/or inefficient handling or ruined by dampness. In the spring of 1945, it was decided to ship some American types directly from the USA to Australia without going through the modification process in the UK. Although this got the aircraft to the main base more quickly than would, otherwise have been the case, it shifted the burden of modifying the aircraft to the latest RN operational standards onto MONAB 2 rather than the better staffed and equipped RDUs in the UK. It added many hundreds of man-hours of work onto their preparation in Australia that negated much of the benefit of direct delivery.

Because the number of aircraft being prepared for service by MONAB 2 never reached the planned totals, there was little work for the Aircraft Storage component and the decision was taken in late February to break it up into four MSRs. Two of these, allocated the numbers 7 and 8 were transferred to the TAMY when it arrived in March. MSR 3 was used to support the replenishment aircraft pools held in *Unicorn* and *Stalker* and MSR 4 was used to augment MONAB 4 at RNAS Ponam.

Despite the slow start, production gathered momentum and when sufficient aircraft were available, they were set up in a flow through the hangars using industrial methods. These involved the breaking down of major tasks into small jobs so that a team could be trained quickly to their task on each aircraft as it 'moved along the line', rather like a modern car factory. The rapid gain in ratings' skill levels enabled the 'dwell time' of aircraft on the hangar floor to be kept to a minimum and production numbers to be increased although the planned wartime target of 125 a month was never reached.

For the first time in the RN, a single Production

Officer was placed in charge of the whole process with air weapon, radio and electrical officers making inputs into a single holistic plan rather than trying to implement their own in isolation. The result was that an aircraft came out of a crate into one hangar and left that same hangar complete in all respects and ready for butt testing, compass swinging and test flight. The results were described in MONAB 2's ROP as "revolutionary" and were fed back into the RN aircraft maintenance and repair organisation across the world. The same search for efficiency led to the discovery that the repair of damaged airframes was not always the best way of getting aircraft into the front line. Damaged aircraft had to undergo extensive scrutiny, were nonstandard in terms of the skills required to make good their defects and did not 'fit' easily into the production lines. That said, if the number of new aircraft delivered into the RDU fell below the total required, more repair work might have to be undertaken to meet the BPF's insatiable appetite for replacement aircraft.

Another new system enabled the Production Officer to analyse progress and inform the stores office of requirements on a day-to-day basis, especially for the really 'hot' items. This greatly reduced the amount of nugatory chasing and gave the best possible outcome from the limited number of components available to the BPF throughout much of 1945. A similar system was introduced throughout the RN after the war and, in developed form, remains in use in the twenty first century.

The production process that evolved at Bankstown was the result of many different inputs. Experience, preconceived ideas about the problems, experiment and improvisation all played their part. The Production officer held daily meetings at which the various section officers analysed the rate of progress on each aircraft. Two basic principles were always adhered to if possible. The first was that any re-adjustment to meet a surge in demand for a particular type must cause the least interference with the general flow. The second was that if one section by doing a small amount of extra work could save another from doing a lot more, it would be instructed to do so. The results were impressive and continued to contribute to the expansion in aircraft delivery numbers. The process

Aircraft lined up at Bankstown awaiting disposal post 1945. In the foreground are Hellcats still in their protective cocoons. Also visible are Vultee Vengeance target tugs of 723 NAS. Along the left edge of the dispersal are the Road/Rail containers used to carry MONAB equipment from the UK to Australia. At Bankstown, once emptied, they were used as offices, stores and workshops.

itself ran like this:

- Aircraft arrived from Sydney docks and were put in the Receipt Park.
- Loose equipment was removed except in aircraft coated in Erenol or in crates.
- The Inspections Section prepared servicing and inspection documents.
- The aircraft was allotted to a hangar for production.
- Whenever possible, aircraft were put in at a steady rate so that no two aircraft reached the same stage at the same time. A "flow" was the object of the exercise so that ordnance, radio and electrical work could be done in turn and without interfering with the airframe and engine work. Specialist parties also incorporated modifications at this stage.

- When it arrived at the end of the hangar line, the inspection section gave the aircraft a final check.
- The aircraft was then moved out of the hangar for an engine run and to have the gun alignment checked if it was a fighter.
- The aircraft was taken to the butts for gun firing and harmonisation.
- Next, it would be taken the compass base for a compass swing and radar equipped aircraft would be checked on the Polar Base for radar alignment.
- The aircraft would be test flown as many times as necessary with any fault rectification necessary being carried out before it was assessed as serviceable.

The Main Naval Stores staff pose for a group photograph on Christmas Day 1945.

- Serviceable aircraft were placed into Category "B" preservation and moved to the Despatch Park. Aircraft with all their internal equipment fitted, ready in all respects for operational service were placed in Category "A" preservation.

The aircraft assembled and test flown in large numbers between February and September included Avengers, Corsairs, Expediters, Fireflies, Hellcats, Martinets, Reliants, Seafires and Sea Otters.

As at Nowra, the Commanding Officer stated in his ROP that much of MONAB 2's equipment was of little value not because of its intrinsic bad quality but because it was not relevant to the static, permanent nature of the RDU function his unit was called upon to perform. Mobile store vans, for instance, were of lit-

tle value given the vast, permanent outfit of stores the RDU actually held and used. What the unit needed was a considerable store of racking to fit into a permanent building. Because MONAB 2 took over a running airfield none of the mobile flying control vehicles were used but the communications equipment including the VHF/DF, YG and JG beacons were set up and worked well. The need to set the many and varied aerials to best advantage led to the CO recommending that the communications team for any future MONAB should be men of "unbounding energy and physical fitness - the open air type".

During the time that Bankstown operated as an RDU 2,500 test flights were carried out with only four major incidents. One of these resulted in the complete write-off of an aircraft with 3 others suffering major

damage. 3 further incidents involved aircraft pitching onto their noses due to the soft state of the airfield surface in wet weather.

723 NAS moved from Nowra and commissioned as a Fleet Requirements Unit on 28 February, taking on charge the aircraft assembled by the advance party. Pending the formation of 724 squadron, 723 operated two Expediter aircraft to set up a communications service between the various naval air stations. As explained in the section on MONAB 1, the squadron did much of its flying from Nowra although it was based at Bankstown.

724 NAS formed at Bankstown on 10 April 1945. It operated as a communications squadron with Expediter and Anson aircraft. These operated from Mascot Airport when the grass surface at Bankstown was unfit for landing and take-off. From the beginning of May the squadron flew a service to Melbourne on five days a week and to Archerfield on three. The service was later expanded to include Maryborough,

Jervis Bay and Nowra. When Bankstown closed, 724 moved to RNAS Schofields.

Because of Bankstown's role as a RDU, it saw few front line squadrons but 1830 and 1833 Corsair squadrons disembarked from *Illustrious* on 14 May 1945. The ship had just left 1 ACS off Okinawa and was about to sail back to the UK for refit. 1830 re-embarked its aircraft for the journey home, 1833's personnel sailed home in their ship but they left their aircraft at Bankstown. 1834 and 1836 squadrons left their Corsairs at Bankstown before their personnel sailed home in *Victorious*.

At its peak in August 1945, the complement of MONAB 2 was 59 officers and 1,373 ratings, of which 1,237 were directly involved in the RDU task for an intended output of 125 aircraft per month. With the end of hostilities, the task of MONAB 2 was gradually run down and it paid off on 31 March 1946, the Bankstown site being handed back to the RAAF.

MONAB 2 sources:

- Report on the Organisation of the Flag Officer Naval Air Pacific in the Archive of the Fleet Air Arm Museum.
- The Development of British Naval Aviation Volume III – unpublished document in the Author's collection.
- The Squadrons of the Fleet Air Arm by Ray Sturtivant & Theo Balance. Published by Air Britain in 1994.
- The Fleet Train by J D Brown. Published in the British Pacific & East Indies Fleet 50th Anniversary Document in 1995.
- *www.faahistoryweb*

Chapter Ten

MONAB 3

HMS Nabthorpe
RNAS Schofields

RNAS Schofields in 1945. The accommodation area to the right gives scale to the image.

The third MONAB began to form at RNAS Ludham on 18 October 1944 under Commander (A) E W Kenton RNVR. It was allowed six weeks to prepare for operational service. As with the first two units, time was spent drawing military clothing, other personal items and in attending lectures on tropical hygiene and airfield defence with sten guns. Technical ratings were sent on courses to equip them to maintain the types of aircraft on which

they were to work. These were expected to be fighters as the Avengers and Barracudas were intended to disembark to Nowra where there was a MATMU to support torpedoes and a suitable range for aircrew to maintain tactical proficiency with weapons. Air engineering components included MM2, MS 3 and MS 4 intended to support Corsairs, Hellcats, Seafires and Fireflies. Like their predecessors, stores personnel struggled whilst at Ludham to receive stores from

Dockyards, identify and re-mark them and then re-pack them in hundreds of cases suitable for the deployment to the Far East. The task was never finished, with resultant confusion in Australia, and Commander Kenton recommended that stores ratings should, in future, begin the work some weeks before the remainder of the MONAB formed up. The majority of personnel were given eight days pre-embarkation leave before they sailed for the Far East in the expectation that it would be some years before they returned to the UK. MONAB 3 commissioned as an independent unit with its own accounts on 4 December 1944 at RNAS Ludham.

Stores had to be collected from the local railway station, where they had been delivered from Dockyards and Depots and then re-consigned to the dockside at Liverpool. The MONAB's transport was pressed into service for this work as soon as it arrived and worked flat out throughout the six-week training period. With no overhaul or preparation for deployment, they were driven to Liverpool and embarked in SS *Essex* dripping wet and bearing the mud of weeks of English winter. Their subsequent state on arrival in Australia can be imagined. The convoy of 89 vehicles and 25 trailers left Ludham for Liverpool on 2 December 1944 led by the Unit's Air Engineering Officer. They had to move through the blackout overnight along roads from which all signposts had been removed lest they help the enemy. There were several accidents and one rating was killed on the journey and two were seriously injured.

On 22 December the ship's company embarked in SS *Athlone Castle*, in Liverpool, after a journey by rail from Ludham and sailed for Australia. Like the previous troopships and transports, both ships sailed via the Panama Canal and crossed the Pacific. Athlone Castle arrived in Sydney on 27 January 1945 and Essex arrived on 4 February. The personnel of MONAB 3

With no tractors available, teams of men had to push aircraft like this Seafire in order to move it, often over unprepared surfaces.

disembarked and moved into tented accommodation at Warwick Farm Racecourse, part of HMS **Golden Hind**. They were to take over and run a new permanent air station being built for the RAAF on the north west outskirts of Sydney at Schofields but, by the end of January, there were no completed accommodation or workshop facilities. An advance party moved in on 5 February and lived, somewhat uneasily, in tented accommodation with the Australian Civilian Construction Corps (CCC) workers. The first runway was handed over complete a day later on 6 February and the advance party erected a Dorland hangar that had been borrowed from RNAS Bankstown, a few miles to the south. As the whole organisation began to move in, huts were handed over for use although they were not yet furnished or provided with electric light.

Tents continued to be used to make up the shortfall and by 10 February it was possible to establish general messing arrangements.

The first aircraft to land at the new air station arrived on 7 February. It was a Stinson Reliant intended for use by the Station Flight. On 10 February, when the fleet carriers arrived in Sydney, the first big disembarkation began and 887 and 894 NAS with Seafires and 1770 NAS with Fireflies disembarked from **Indefatigable**. The squadron personnel lived in tents and the last sailors moved into Schofields from Warwick Farm on 18 February. Schofields grew rapidly into a major naval air station, with a task similar to many in the UK, literally overnight and was able, only just in time, to support the BPF. The provision of amenities had not been high on the list of initial prior-

Another view of RNAS Schofields in 1945.

ities but the Australian authorities helped enormously by laying on special trains from Quakers' Hill to take libertymen into Sydney about 35 miles distant. The 'amenities' van, part of the original MONAB package, proved most useful and a large tent was set up by the YMCA, in which sailors could have a quiet moment or write letters home. An open-air cinema and a "primitive" beer bar were also set up in the first days. MONAB 3 formally commissioned as HMS *Nabthorpe*, RNAS Schofields on 18 February 1945, over a week after the first squadrons had disembarked.

On 23 February 1840 NAS Hellcats disembarked from *Speaker* adding to the flying task and the number of aircraft types to be supported. On the same day the vehicles began to arrive, having been made as driveable as possible by the RAAF in Sydney. The RAAF transport organisation also started to deliver the hundreds of stores boxes. The workshop lorries were set up as intended in the open but the amount of dust created on what was still very much a building site, limited their practical usefulness. A second Dorland hangar was borrowed from Bankstown and set up as a temporary workshop. *Indefatigable's* squadrons re-embarked on 27 February, easing some of the accommodation problems.

885 NAS with Seafires and 1772 NAS with Fireflies disembarked from *Ruler* on 18 March and brought the number of squadrons disembarked at the base to six. Like the earlier MONABs, it had never operated as a temporary base and was, to all intents and purposes, a permanent naval air station intended to provide support for disembarked front-line squadrons. The mobile workshops and facilities came in for criticism but it was understood that they were performing a task that was far more extensive than that for which they had been intended. Further, until the permanent facilities were complete, they were all that RNAS Schofields had.

On 10 April, 706 NAS commissioned as a pool for operational aircrew and refresher flying school. It had begun to form at Jervis Bay but moved to Schofields in March. It was a large unit with 36 aircraft, 6 each of the six types operated by the BPF - Corsair, Hellcat, Seafire, Firefly, Avenger and Barracuda. The latter type formed part of the light fleet carrier air groups

that arrived in Australia from July 1945. The squadron moved to Maryborough on 28 August and began to reduce in size although its task remained unaltered.

899 NAS with Seafires disembarked from *Chaser* on 23 April 1945 and 1843 NAS with Corsairs disembarked from *Arbiter* on 1 May. Work to complete the base continued as quickly as possible and by June 1945 it accommodated 200 officers and 1400 ratings. In that month, however, progress was severely hampered by heavy rain that led to flooding and acres of mud. To add to these problems, industrial disputes led to strikes involving the CCC labour force. Despite these handicaps, 899 NAS began to run the first conversion course for RAAF officers who had volunteered to transfer to the RANVR in order to fly in the Fleet Air Arm.

In May 1945, 1843 NAS disembarked its Corsairs from *Arbiter* and there were parties to celebrate the end of the war in Europe. The second big disembarkation period followed in June when 1 ACS returned to Sydney for a logistic re-supply period. *Indefatigable's* air group comprising 887 and 894 NAS with Seafires, 1770 NAS with Fireflies and 820 NAS with Avengers came ashore on 5 June. While the group was at Schofields, 1772 NAS replaced 1770, also with Fireflies and the re-structured air group became 7 Carrier Air Group (CAG). This was part of the policy of adopting USN style air groups, which could be replaced in carriers when necessary by "spare" air groups to reduce aircrew fatigue. 1834 and 1836 NAS disembarked their Corsairs from *Victorious* during the same period, re-embarking on 26 June. 7 CAG re-embarked on 7 July for operations off the mainland of Japan. Schofields remained busy as four new light fleet carriers arrived in Australia, doubling the number of large carriers in the BPF. 15 CAG, comprising 1851 NAS with Corsairs and 814 NAS Barracudas disembarked from *Venerable* on 21 July.

Admiral Sir Bruce Fraser, the Commander-in-Chief BPF, visited RNAS Schofields on 28 July 1945, by which time the base was nearly complete. Air group moves continued with 15 CAG re-embarking on 13 August and the night-fighter Fireflies of 1790 NAS disembarking from *Vindex* on VJ Day, 15 August. 16

CAG, comprising 1831 and 837 NAS disembarked from *Glory* on 16 August and 880 NAS with Seafires disembarked from *Implacable* on 25 August.

The training squadron, 706 NAS, moved to RNAS Maryborough on 28 August as part of a rationalisation of BPF support facilities in Australia. 1770 NAS followed them a day later and 16 CAG re-embarked on 1 September. A new training squadron arrived on 4 September. This was 702 NAS, an instrument training and standards unit that had formed at RNAS Hinstock in the UK in 1944 and travelled to Australia by sea with its Oxford and Harvard aircraft.

801 NAS disembarked from *Implacable* on 9 September. With the rundown of the BPF already gathering momentum, 880 NAS disbanded two days later, some of its personnel and aircraft being absorbed into 801, some from both units starting the demobilisation process. The very successful courses run for RANVR officers in 899 NAS ended after the second group of twelve qualified and the squadron disbanded on 18 September.

MONAB 3 paid off on 15 November 1945, its personnel being drafted back to the UK for demobilisation and to other MONABs and units within the BPF. The task of running RNAS Schofields in support of disembarked operational squadrons was taken on by MONAB 6 on the same date.

MONAB 3 sources:

- Report on the Organisation of the Flag Officer Naval Air Pacific in the Archive of the Fleet Air Arm Museum.
- The Development of British Naval Aviation Volume III – unpublished manuscript in the Author's Collection.
- The Squadrons of the Fleet Air Arm by Ray Sturtivant & Theo Balance. Published by Air Britain in 1994.
- The Flight of the Pelican – History of Schofields Aerodrome & Quakers' Hill by Ron Robb. Published by *HMAS Nirimba* Welfare Committee in 1993.
- *www.faahistoryweb*

Chapter Eleven

MONAB 4

HMS Nabaron
RNAS Ponam

The accommodation area to the northwest of Ponam Island. Note the cinema with its log seats, centre right of the picture.

This was the best documented of the mobile air bases for, in addition to the Reports of Proceeding (ROP) contained in the Report on FONAP's Organisation in the Fleet Air Arm Museum's Archive, there are also a number of personal diaries. From the latter it appears that ratings began to come together at their drafting Port Divisions before moving to RNAS Ludham for training. Thus FAA ratings gathered at RNAS Lee-on-Solent and supply ratings at HMS *Drake* in Devonport. They moved to RNAS Ludham on 15 November 1944, shortly before MONAB 1 left and with the personnel of MONABs 2 and 3 still working up. The intensity of the 'pipeline' can be gathered from the fact that MONAB 5, in turn, began to form before MONAB 4 embarked.

Ludham had been laid out by the RAF on a dispersed principle with buildings and facilities spread out around the perimeter rather than concentrated with the consequent vulnerability to air attack. The extreme

winter conditions in 1944/45 made the routine of forming up difficult with ratings forced to queue for hours for equipment, meals or inoculations in rain or snow. The former airfield was a large grass area, which was used as a vehicle park and for tented camps to house MONAB personnel. It became a morass. Technical components include MA 1, MM 3, MS 5 and MS 6 intended to support Avenger, Firefly, Seafire, Corsair and Hellcat aircraft.

MONAB 4 commissioned on 1 January 1945 as HMS *Nabaron*, an independent command with its own accounts. All MONABs were given ship's names beginning with the letters "Nab" but there is more detail on the selection of this one. The first commanding officer was Captain A N C Bingley OBE RN, known throughout the Service as 'Baron' Bingley. The name, therefore, was chosen to reflect the colourful personality of the unit's captain. The extent to which the 'Baron' was involved in the selection of the

Erecting a mobile radar unit.

name is not recorded.

MONAB 4's vehicles, equipment and personnel left Ludham on 16 January 1945 for Liverpool, the personnel travelling by train. On arrival, they embarked in the troopship SS **Dominion Monarch** while the vehicles and stores were loaded into the slower SS **Clan Macauley**. The troopship joined a convoy with 27 other merchant ships and sailed west across the Atlantic with an escort of cruisers and destroyers. They left the convoy and proceeded alone on 25 January, changing into white uniforms off Puerto Rico on 30 January. They passed through the Panama Canal on 3 February and arrived in Sydney after crossing the Pacific on 21 February. A day later they moved into tented accommodation at Warwick Farm Racecourse, part of RN Barracks, Sydney HMS Golden Hind. The ratings described the tented transit camp as a "wonderful place to stay" especially since the food, which included steak, ice cream and fresh

fruit, was "excellent", the only time I have seen that adjective used by a sailor when describing food! Heads of Department and other senior officers were accommodated in Sydney where they could liase easily with FONAP staff officers. Once ashore, the sight of fruit that had not been seen in Britain since 1939 including pineapples, bananas, melons, nectarines and much more overwhelmed the sailors. Supply Assistant Bernard Brown bought passion fruit but threw it away because "it was full of seeds" and he didn't like the look of it! Like thousands of others, he was given the name of a host family in Sydney and spent a weekend with the Merediths. To many sailors this must have seemed a wonderful experience and a considerable number came back to Australia as emigrants after the war. While they waited for the move to an operational airfield, the ratings followed a normal barrack routine with rounds, divisions, church parades, queues for inoculations and the issue of pay,

The shower facility in use.

Sunday divisions.

Vengeance Fleet Requirements aircraft of 721 NAS parked on the disperal area.

rum and clothing coupons. ENSA shows and the cinema were popular in the evening. With an eye to the immediate future, Bernard Brown bought a book on Pacific islands.

While it had been on passage to Australia, the decision had been taken to use MONAB 4 to man an airfield built by a USN Construction Battalion on Ponam in the Admiralty Islands north of New Guinea. The decision was taken too late redirect *Dominion Monarch* but the stores ship *Clan Macauley* was diverted and lay off Manus, the largest of the Admiralty Islands waiting to be unloaded. An advance party from MONAB 4, including the newly attached MSR 4, was sent from Sydney to begin the task of unloading *Clan Macauley*. They arrived at Ponam Island on 13 March 1945. On 22 March SS *Fort Edmonton* arrived with three months' victualling stores which were unloaded by the advance party. With considerable help from the CB detachment left on Ponam by the USN, all domestic services were working when the main party arrived from Sydney. Food was in short supply at first and the problem was not finally solved until a major delivery of victualling stores by the RFAs *Fort Dunvegan* and *Fort Alabama* at the end of July. The maximum number victualled on Ponam was 1180 in mid June 1945.

The USN had built the airfield on Ponam after the island's capture in 1944. It was handed over to the Royal Navy complete with all services including a fresh water desalination system, hospital, dining halls, officers' club and Quonset huts for accommodation. There were also generating and refrigerating plants

and a huge petrol storage unit. A CB unit of one officer and 40 men was left by the USN to maintain the airfield and domestic services for the British.

The work of unloading proved extremely difficult since the ship had not been 'combat loaded' and stores for other destinations lay on top of the MONAB equipment in the holds. Had it not been for extensive help from the USN, it might not have proved possible to unload *Clan Macauley* without sending her to docks in Australia to be emptied and reloaded. The main party embarked in SS *Empire Arquebus* on 16 March and sailed for Ponam, arriving on 24 March. HMS *Nabaron* re-commissioned formally as RNAS Ponam on 2 April 1945. It became operational almost immediately with disembarkation of six Corsairs from *Unicorn*. On 30 April two Avengers and four spare Avenger crews were disembarked from *Fencer*. These formed the beginning of a forward pool of replacement aircraft for the BPF and keeping them in serviceable condition allowed the replacement air-

crew, when they arrived, to stay in current flying practice. Forty operational aircraft were delivered by the ferry carriers before the end of May.

The flying task increased considerably in May. A Fleet Requirements Unit (FRU), 721 NAS equipped with Vengeance aircraft and an Air Search and Rescue (ASR) unit, 1701 NAS 'B' Flight with Sea Otter amphibians were landed from *Begum* on 28 May. The Vengeances were used to act as targets for air interceptions and towed drogues for air to air firings, forming a vital aspect of Ponam's ability to keep replacement aircraft and aircrew in a fit state to join the carrier squadrons when required. 1701B remained operational until the end of August but was never called on to carry out a rescue. On 29 May *Implacable* arrived off Ponam and for a further six weeks her aircraft used the airfield to carry out ADDLs and general flying training. MSR 6 arrived on 1 June to help with the aircraft replenishment task.

On 19 June 885 NAS disembarked from *Ruler* to

The open air cinema.

A Corsair being manhandled into a maintainance area. It has East Indies Fleet markings, and has yet to be sprayed with the BPF roundel and bar.

carry out a week of intensive interception, strafing, air to air firing and ADDLs for its relatively inexperienced pilots. It re-embarked on 28 June, after which 1 ACS worked up in the Manus areas following its logistic re-supply period in Sydney, prior to operations off the Japanese mainland. Aircraft from **Formidable**, **Victorious** and **Vengeance** disembarked for short periods. MATMU 7 was disembarked from SS **Clan Chattan** on 6 July. In addition to the large carriers, the ferry and replenishment carriers were frequent visitors to load and unload aircraft. RFAs including **Fort Dunvegan**, **Fort Langley** and **Fort Colville** in addition to the Norwegian ships **Slegvig** and **Kistmas** carried out the build up of stores in July and early August. **Pioneer** arrived on 19 July to deliver another aircraft lighter and stores and **Unicorn** paid a brief visit on 31 July to embark damaged aircraft returned from the fleet for repairs.

RNAS Ponam rapidly developed a routine that would be familiar on RN Air Stations throughout the world. Three times a week a launch or landing craft went to the larger island of Manus to collect mail and stores. RAF Dakotas from Australia were frequent

visitors with passengers, mail and urgent stores. They were the largest aircraft to use the airfield during this period. The daily routine was

0530	Call the Hands
0600	Hands to breakfast
0630	Church
0700	Commence work
1015	Stand easy until 1030
1200	Secure, hands to dinner
1400	Commence work
1600	Secure, hands to tea
1800	Up spirits
1830	Hands to supper
2100	Messdeck rounds
	Pipe down

Nabaron had its own newspaper, the "Jungle Echo" which included world and local news with the local sports results from inter-departmental football and cricket matches. On 29 April it had been able to record that a single Japanese aircraft had bombed Manus at 2 o'clock in the morning. The supply of sufficient paper

for the Echo proved difficult, however and it would have had to cease production in mid June if paper had not been obtained in quantity from the USN. There was little for the sailors to spend their money on and the ship's company deposited £5,012/12/6d in the Post Office Savings Bank by the end of April, a lot for a relatively small unit.

June 1945 saw a further seventy-two replacement aircraft delivered and forty-four embarked in replenishment carriers for issue to the 1st Aircraft Carrier Squadron. The month also saw Ponam's only fatal accidents. A Vengeance of 721 NAS experienced a control restriction while taking off on 12 June and crashed in the lagoon killing the pilot, Lieutenant Kirby. On 20 June a Seafire of 880 NAS from *Implacable* crashed into a radio mast after an ADDL session and burnt. Sub Lieutenant Peter Record, the pilot, died some hours later in the Sick Bay. Both men

were buried at sea from the deck of an aircraft lighter, both ceremonies being marred by the discovery that the unit's only bugler was unable to sound off either the Last Post or Reveille. In his ROP the commanding officer observed for the benefit of the Drafting Office that "when the number of buglers borne is only one, a proficient rating ought to be provided".

On 4 July the commanding officer, Captain Bingley was taken ill. He made no improvement and was evacuated to the RN Hospital at Herne Bay in Sydney on 17 July. He was relieved in command by Acting Commander W S Thomas DSC RN. FONAP visited RNAS Ponam on 1 August, together with the Commodore Air Train, the Staff Engineer Officer and Flag Lieutenant. They stayed overnight and discussed progress in establishing the airfield as the BPF's forward base. The monotony of work on the island and the poor food available were mentioned and shortly

Work on the Twin Wasp R-2800-8 engine of a Corsair being carried out in the open.

after FONAP's return to Australia steps were taken to improve both. On 15 August, before news of the Japanese surrender arrived, an aircraft delivered a quantity of fresh fruit and took off to return to Australia with libertymen. RAFT visited the base in his flagship *Montclare* on 8 August. Twelve Corsairs and 6 Barracudas were disembarked from *Vengeance* on 28 August with 52 officers and 43 ratings. They re-embarked two days later after a period of flying training.

On 30 August Captain C J Blake RN arrived to assume command.

After VJ Day, Ponam was put at one month's notice for closure. As RNFAP 1 on Pityilu was ordered to close down in early September, its aircraft were flown to Ponam and *Unicorn* evacuated the unit itself on 17 September. During September the MONAB presence on Ponam was run down with MSR 6 embarked in *Vindex* on 26 September for return to Australia and a number of ships, including SS *Fernmoor*, arrived to load with naval and air stores. Opportunities were also taken to embark some aircraft and personnel in every ship that had capacity. The flying task continued, however, with Corsairs from 1841 NAS in *Formidable* and 1850 NAS in *Vengeance* using the airfield for short periods. Barracudas of 812 NAS disembarked from the latter carrier for a short rest period. By the end of August £21,400 had been deposited in the National Savings Bank.

On 3 October *Reaper* arrived to embark 1701B NAS with its Sea Otters and on 6 October *Unicorn* returned to pick up 721 NAS and MRS 4 together with a large quantity of crated air stores. She sailed on 9 October when SS *Charmain* arrived to embark the MATMU and its vehicles. The drawdown of MONAB personnel had begun on 7 October when an advance party, including the chaplain, embarked in Ariadne for passage to Australia. *Unicorn* returned for a further load on 24 October and work started early the next morning to load her with the MONAB's G1098 equipment including beds and office equipment. The 150th and last edition of the "Jungle Echo" was printed on 22 October as RNAS Ponam was made ready to be handed back to the USN. *Chaser* arrived on 30 October and sailed a day later with personnel of MMU 5 and

two Walrus aircraft. The last MONAB personnel moved onboard *Unicorn* on 28 October and, after loading yet more stores, she sailed on 31 October some hours later than *Chaser*. A small rear-guard returned the airfield and its equipment to the USN CBs on 9 November.

Once in Sydney on 6 November, MONAB 4 effectively ceased to exist and after helping to unload medical, victualling and air stores, ratings were drafted back to the UK or to air stations and ships that were remaining in the Pacific. Bernard Brown went to *Slinger* with a draft that was returning to the UK. They sailed from Sydney on 10 November and proceeded to the UK via Fremantle, Colombo, the Suez Canal and Gibraltar. They arrived in time for Christmas leave.

The experience of *Nabaron* at Ponam might be thought to vindicate the original concept of the MONAB, able to operate on a tropical island with minimal outside help. This would be a false impression, however, since the unit could not have functioned without the work carried out by the SeaBees before they arrived and in support after they arrived. Much of the equipment brought out from the UK remained unused, notably the tents intended for accommodation and generators to provide electrical power. Other equipment provided generously by the USN had no equivalent in the British outfit of stores but without it, the air station could not have functioned. For example heavy lifting equipment and cranes; machines for making and repairing runways and roads; refrigerators and a parachute packing room with a de-humidifier. In fact the airfield MONAB 4 took over on Ponam had semi-permanent features better than many of those other MONABs found on airfields in Australia. Like them, the unit found itself operating as a permanent naval air station and not as a mobile one. Without the use of USN lifting equipment, for instance, no aircraft could have been transferred from ship to shore by lighter or vice versa. Even then, the US "A" Frame crane was incapable of lifting a Barracuda and so supporting the aircraft embarked in the light fleet carriers would have been problematical had it been necessary.

Flying from Ponam was straightforward as it came

fully equipped with a control tower and workshops. The former was fitted with British radio sets and other equipment removed from the mobile control vans. *Unicorn* left six Corsairs ashore on her first visit but since Lieutenant Commander 'Flying' was the only pilot at that time, he had to carry out all test and routine flying. More pilots were urgently needed and eventually arrived. The MONAB's allowance of stores included three pilot-type parachutes but these had not been supplied and when the number of pilots increased to four, flying had to be fitted around borrowed parachutes for these newcomers. Air engineering suffered from the inevitable shortage of spares, tools and equipment. The lack of hangarage meant that aircraft had to be worked on in the open in between heavy showers of rain. They had to be flown often, preferably daily, to keep them dry internally. The movements of the fleet and replenishment carriers followed no fixed pattern leading to peaks and troughs of activity that impacted on the workload of the maintainers. This was not unique to Ponam.

Ponam was crucial to the long term plans to deploy an expanding BPF in operations against Japan. Although the fleet returned to Australia for replacement aircraft in the June 1945 replenishment, heavy demands would have been made on the forward replacement pools on Ponam and Pityilu had Operation Olympic gone ahead as planned. Demand might well have exceeded the number of airframes available.

A summary of aircraft transactions gives a good idea of Ponam's success in achieving its aim.

	Received	Despatched
May	40	0
June	72	44
July	6	53
August	48	28
September	45	52

In the last edition of the Jungle Echo, Captain Blake wrote:

"During my time here I have been very favourably impressed with the way in which not only the Nabaron Departments but all attached units have worked harmoniously together while still retaining their individuality. The Nabaron spirit is a good one so take it with you to your next job whether in the Service or in "civvy street". Although when you are crossing Stonehouse Bridge in the cold rain, you may not actually wish yourself back in Ponam, you will I hope, always remember Nabaron as a good ship in which to have served. Goodbye to Ponam, good luck to you all."

C J Blake
Captain Royal Navy

MONAB 4 sources:

- Diary of SA Bernard Brown in the Archive of the Fleet Air Arm Museum.
- Report on the Organisation of the Flag Officer Naval Air Pacific in the Archive of the Fleet Air Arm Museum.
- Report on the Experience of the British Pacific Fleet – 1946 in the Archive of the Fleet Air Arm Museum.
- The Squadrons of the Fleet Air Arm by Ray Sturtivant & Theo balance. Published by Air Britain in 1994.
- The Development of British Naval Aviation Volume III. Unpublished manuscript in the Author's Collection.
- The Fleet Train by J D Brown, part of the British Pacific & East Indies Fleet "Forgotten Fleets" 50th Anniversary Publication 1995.
- *www.faahistoryweb*

Chapter Twelve

MONAB 5

HMS Nabswick
RNAS Jervis Bay
RNAS Nowra

RNAS Jervis Bay.

MONAB 5 began to form on 28 December 1944 under Captain H G Dickinson DSC RN. It originally included an MR component but this was withdrawn on 11 January 1945 and MM 4, MS 7 and 8 together with MSR 1 and 2 components were substituted. Between them, the components were to be capable of storing and maintaining the five types of aircraft in operational service with the BPF plus the Martinet TT 1 target tug. The changes led to considerable re-drafting and a number of ratings joined only a few days before sailing from the UK. Few had been given pre-embarkation leave and the rectification of this oversight was given priority. In consequence, training on aircraft and equipment was inadequate and there were too few ratings to make up sufficient stores handling parties. Another problem involved drivers, many of whom turned out to be unable to drive on arrival at Ludham. Worse, they had

been drafted against the original complement of 88 vehicles but by the time MONAB 5 formed 122 had been allocated. HMS *Nabswick* commissioned as a self-accounting unit at RNAS Ludham on 1 February 1945 perpetuating, through no fault of its people, many of the same problems that its predecessors had struggled to overcome. None of the earlier units had yet found time to feed experience back into the training system.

The vehicles themselves caused particular problems, many of them arriving too late to be serviced before embarkation. Indeed, some of them were so late that they joined the convoy of vehicles as it made its way from Ludham to Liverpool! These included the radio vans which, in consequence, were not checked or test-

ed until they arrived in Australia. The late arrival of the diesel generators meant that the mobile workshops could not be tested either. Again, the thousands of crates containing stores overwhelmed the small and inexperienced party of stores ratings. Stores officers had to use their judgement over questions of how much cash, loan clothing and "compo" rations should be demanded in the absence of any form of guidance. Some of the stores were sent from depots uncrated for overseas shipment. These and a considerable quantity of items listed on Army Form G 1098 such as beds and office furniture had to be cased or crated after acceptance, before being despatched to Liverpool.

The personnel left Ludham on the night of 16 February and embarked in SS *Stirling Castle* in

RNAS Jervis Bay dispersal area.

The workshop area under construction. Note the half finished Dorland hangar in the background.

Liverpool on 18 February 1945 together with the personnel of TAMY 1. The vehicles and stores sailed a week later in SS *Durham*. As with previous deployments, both ships sailed for Australia via the Panama Canal. *Stirling Castle* arrived in Sydney on 29 March and MONAB 5 underwent several changes. Captain Dickinson transferred to command MONAB 1 at Nowra and was relieved in MONAB 5 by Acting

Parked Avengers and Reliants after VJ Day.

A further aerial view of RNAS Jervis Bay.

Commander T K Masterman RN. Both MSR components were detached to form part of MONAB 1 on arrival and the remainder of the personnel moved into accommodation at Nowra where they unloaded the stores and equipment and, after checking it, moved it to Jervis Bay ready for use. They found that some of the stores were damaged, especially crates that were marked NAAFI and the task of finding and identifying over 5,000 crates on the dockside took some days.

MONAB 5 re-commissioned as HMS *Nabswick*, RNAS Jervis Bay on 1 May 1945 with Captain Dickinson resuming command. The airfield was intended to support the BPF by providing disembarked aviation facilities for the fleet's front line squadrons while their parent carriers were in harbour. Like previous MONABs, Number 5 effectively ceased to be mobile when it took responsibility for a semi-permanent air station in the main base area of Australia. Despite the limited nature of its support facilities it fulfilled pretty much the same functions that an air station in the UK was required to carry out. Because of the limited facilities, reliance had to be placed on the mobile equipment brought from the UK, including four Dorland hangars. The latter proved

vulnerable to high winds and some ingenuity had to be put into improving their tethering arrangements. The officers made use of accommodation at the nearby RAN College.

Fireflies of 1771 NAS and Avengers of 828 NAS from HMS *Implacable* flew into Jervis Bay on 7 May followed a day later by the carrier's two Seafire squadrons, 801 and 880. The first two re-embarked on 24 May followed on 25 May by the Seafires. On 1 June HMS *Formidable's* air group comprising 1841 and 1842 Corsair squadrons and 848 squadron's Avengers disembarked. They re-embarked on 22 June. 723 Fleet requirements squadron, which had been at Jervis Bay since before *Nabswick* arrived, moved back to Nowra on 4 June.

On 12 July 1843 Corsair squadron moved to Jervis bay from RAAF Maryborough. It was intended to form part of the new "spare" carrier air group which was to form up at Nowra ready to replace one of long-serving air groups at sea. It relocated to Nowra on 20 July. Two days later the air group from the new light fleet carrier *Colossus* disembarked for continuation flying. This comprised the Barracudas of 812 NAS and the Corsairs of 1846 NAS. On the same day Barracudas of 827 NAS and Corsairs of 1850 NAS disembarked from a second light fleet carrier, *Vengeance*. Both air groups re-embarked on 13 August. A quiet period followed during which VJ Day was celebrated. On 11 September a third light fleet carrier, HMS *Glory* disembarked the Barracudas of 837 NAS and Corsairs of 1831 NAS. 837 transferred to Nowra on 29 October.

After VJ Day the BPF began to disband squadrons and run down the scale of its operations in Australia. In consequence MONAB 5 de-commissioned Jervis Bay on 14 November 1945 and handed the station back to the RAAF. A day later it replaced MONAB 1 and re-commissioned RNAS Nowra releasing higher priority personnel to return to the UK for demobilisation. Captain J F H Sawyer RN assumed command on 18 November.

1831 NAS moved from Jervis Bay to Nowra with MONAB 5 and joined 820, 828 and 837 NAS which were already disembarked there. 820 re-embarked in *Indefatigable* on 23 November and 1831 was reduced in size from 21 aircraft to 12 on 26 November. 837 NAS re-embarked in *Glory* on 14 January 1946 followed by 1831 NAS on 19 January. By then Nowra itself was being run down ready to be handed back to the RAAF and 723 NAS moved to RNAS Schofields leaving 828 as the last remaining RN squadron.

In February 1946 the ship's company of HMS *Nabswick* marched through the streets of Nowra to thank the local population for the support they had given the Royal Navy over the previous year and to say goodbye. MONAB 5 paid off on 18 March and Nowra returned to RAAF control. 828 NAS remained as lodger unit for two months and then the personnel sailed home in *HMS Implacable*, leaving their aircraft behind to be destroyed. MONAB 5 personnel joined other BPF units or made their way back to the UK for demobilisation.

MONAB 5 sources:

- Report on the Organisation of the Flag Officer Naval Air Pacific in the Archive of the Fleet Air Arm Museum.
- The Squadrons of the Fleet Air Arm by Ray Sturtivant & Theo Balance. Published by Air Britain in 1994.
- *www.faahistoryweb*

Chapter Thirteen

MONAB 6

HMS Nabstock
RAAF Maryborough

Hangars and aircraft dispersal at RAAF Maryborough.

After MONAB 5 and TAMY 1 had formed, the MNAO moved from RNAS Ludham to Middle Wallop, which was taken over from the RAF specifically for the purpose. The name HMS *Flycatcher* was retained.

Personnel for MONAB 6 began to assemble at RNAS Middle Wallop on 1 March 1945. The technical components comprised MM 5 intended to maintain Avengers, Corsairs, Hellcats and Seafires; MS 9 to service Avengers; MS 10 to service Vengeance target

tugs and MR 2 to hold quantities of reserve Avengers and second line types including Expeditors, Sea Otters and Martinet target tugs.

Despite the six months experience that preceded its formation, MONAB 6 was forced to cope with the familiar problems of giving leave, training the untrained and trying to cope with the overwhelming problem of identifying and cataloguing stores. There was still no standard inventory against which the issues could be compared. Again, replacements had to

be found for sailors who were found to be too old or unfit for foreign service on joining.

HMS Nabstock commissioned as a self-accounting unit under Captain H V P McClintock DSC RN on 1 April 1945. Most of the personnel travelled by train to Greenock on the Clyde on 20 April to embark in SS *Nieuw Amsterdam*. They sailed for Sydney, via the Panama Canal on 22 April. The movement of vehicles and stores was made even more complicated than usual by being loaded into three separate merchant ships, SS *Trojan*, SS *Empire Splendour* and SS *Empire Captain*. They sailed from Sandown Docks on 1 May 1945. *Nieuw Amsterdam* arrived in Sydney on 23 May; the slower stores ships did not arrive until 14 June. Most of the sailors moved into the usual tented accommodation at Warwick Farm.

Captain McClintock together with Commander Wilson, Commander Coote, Commander Kennet and Lieutenant Commander Lavers had flown to Australia to find a base suitable for MONAB 6. On 19 May they travelled to RAAF Maryborough near Brisbane and assessed it as a suitable temporary base. The decision was taken to move in as a lodger unit, pending the availability of a naval air station and an advance party of sailors arrived from Sydney on 24 May followed by a second batch on 28 May. Although MONAB 6 had originally been intended to provide airfield support for disembarked front line squadrons and spare air groups as they formed, it was now intended to hold a stock of replacement aircraft for issue to the replenishment carriers. A Corsair, the first aircraft to arrive, landed on 29 May 1945 and the unit's vehicles began to arrive in late June, having been repaired in Sydney. Maryborough remained on RAAF charge with a radar school and other units continuing to function.

MONAB 6 re-commissioned as HMS *Nabstock* at RAAF Maryborough on 1 June 1945 in a ceremony attended by Rear Admiral Portal, the FONAP. Unlike its predecessors, it retained much of its mobile status and was expected to move on when a more suitable base was identified. The first aircraft to disembark to Maryborough were the Fireflies of 1770 NAS from HMS *Indefatigable* on 6 June. On 15 June, the Sea Otters of A Flight 1701 NAS disembarked from HMS *Begum* for SAR duties from shore bases. On 23 June

1845 NAS flew its Corsairs from the TAMY at Archerfield to Maryborough followed on 4 July by another Corsair squadron, 1843, which disembarked from HMS *Arbiter*. Both left on 24 July, 1845 for Nowra and 1843 for Jervis Bay. Seafires of 899 NAS operated as a detachment to Maryborough between 24 and 27 July when the first conversion course of former RAAF pilots carried out their deck landing training on HMS *Indomitable*.

After VJ Day a complicated series of squadron movements followed the decision to run down the BPF. 1834 and 1836 NAS disembarked their Corsairs from *Victorious* on 23 August, together with the Avengers of 849 NAS. The latter flew on to Mascot airfield in Sydney on the next day. 1834 and 1836 flew their aircraft to Bankstown for disposal in early September and the personnel then embarked in *Victorious* for passage to the UK and demobilisation. 706 NAS moved to Maryborough from Schofields on 28 August followed by 1770 NAS Fireflies on 29 August. 899 operated a second detachment between 10 and 13 September when the second course of Australian pilots carried out their DLTs on *Arbiter*.

706 NAS, much reduced in size, relocated to Nowra on 24 October and naval flying operations ceased on the same day. MONAB 6 then began to move men and equipment to Schofields where they took over from MONAB 3, which was to be demobilised. *HMS Nabstock* formally ended its lodger status at Maryborough on 14 November 1945 and re-commissioned at RNAS Schofields, keeping its same ship's name on 15 November. A retard party stayed at Maryborough to wind down the RN facilities and hand them back to the RAAF. The last RN personnel left Maryborough in December.

Schofields was still a busy air station in December 1945 with 702, 1772, 1790, 801, 885, 887, 894 squadrons disembarked and carrying out full flying programmes. Two Corsair squadrons, 1850 from *Vengeance* and 1851 from *Venerable* disembarked in January 1946, re-embarking in March and February respectively. There were no more disembarkations after January 1946 and the squadrons gradually returned to their parent carriers and MONAB 6 began to run down its operations at Schofields. The last

squadron to leave was 1790 with its night fighter Fireflies which embarked on *Implacable* on 5 April 1946 for passage to the UK. With the end of the flying task, stores and equipment were either returned to depot or destroyed and the size of the ship's company was steadily reduced as men were returned to the UK for demobilisation. Surplus equipment was allegedly burnt and the ashes dumped in the bush. MONAB 6, and with it RNAS Schofields, paid off on 9 June 1946 and the airfield was returned formally to the RAAF.

*Corsair fighters flown ashore to MONAB 6 from **Victorious** and **Formidable** await disposal in September 1946.*

MONAB 6 sources:

- Report on the Organisation of the Flag Officer Naval Air Pacific in the Archive of the Fleet Air Arm Museum.
- The Squadrons of the Fleet Air Arm by Ray Sturtivant & Theo Balance. Published by Air Britain in 1994.
- The Flight of the Pelican – history of Schofields Aerodrome & Quakers Hill by Ron Robb. Published by ***HMAS Nirimba*** Welfare Committee in 1993.
- The Development of British Naval Aviation. Unpublished manuscript in the Author's Collection.
- *www.faahistoryweb*

Chapter Fourteen

MONAB 7

HMS Nabreekie
RNAS Archerfield

RNAS Archerfield with the Kerry Road workshops at the top of the picture.

MONAB 7 began to assemble at RNAS Middle Wallop on 19 March 1945. It was intended to be a second Receipt and Dispatch Unit (RDU) for operation from a forward base but it lacked the MSR components that had formed part of MONAB 2. It had Equipping and Stripping Units instead. The components on formation included MM 6 to support Avenger, Corsair, Hellcat and Seafire aircraft; MS 11 to support Fireflies and MS 12 to support Sea Otters which were intended to give SAR cover in the operational area. There was

an Erection & Equipping Unit tasked to prepare Avenger, Corsair, Hellcat, Seafire, Sea Otter and Vengeance aircraft. The Stripping Unit was capable of reducing all these aircraft to 'produce' with the exception of the Vengeance target tug which was also in service with RAAF and which service could, if necessary, provide support.

HMS *Nabreekie* commissioned as an independent unit holding its own accounts under Captain F P Frai RNVR on 1 June 1945. The ship's name is believed to be a second example of commanding officer's influ-

ence since Captain Frai was a native of Edinburgh - "auld reekie". Again, it is not certain if the captain chose the name or if it was selected for him. It was originally to have been named *Nabsfield*.

After the usual tribulations with transport, stores and leave arrangements whilst forming up, the unit personnel travelled to Liverpool by train on 19 June and embarked in two troop ships, the SS *Stirling Castle* and SS *Andes*. Both sailed on 21 June 1945. In addition to the naval parties, both carried Australian and New Zealand servicemen who had been prisoners of war in Germany. The vehicles and stores sailed in SS *Samfoyle* from the Gladstone Dock in Liverpool several days later. All three ships passed through the Panama Canal but differed from their predecessors in stopping at Wellington to discharge the New Zealanders after their journey home. The Australians were landed in Sydney with MONAB 7 when the troopships arrived there on 28 July. There being no airfield ready to accept the latest MONAB, personnel moved into tented accommodation at Newcastle race course, another component of HMS *Golden Hind*. By that stage, the decision had been taken not to deploy a RDU to the Philippines and experience with MONAB 2 showed how difficult it would be to make such a task mobile. MONAB 7 was, therefore, not to be used in

its intended role and the decision was taken to retain it in Australia. In the short term it was decided to locate *Nabreekie* at RNAS Archerfield with TAMY 1 and move it to a new air station as soon as one became available. The decision was taken in time to divert *Samfoyle* to Brisbane in order to unload the unit's stores nearer their destination.

While the bulk of the personnel awaited developments, a detachment of 50 were lent to the TAMY to help with the erection of Seafire aircraft at RAAF Oakey in Queensland. The main body travelled by train to the RN Establishment at Rocklea, just north of Archerfield in August. HMS *Nabreekie* re-commissioned at RN Camp Rocklea on 8 August 1945. On 10 August about 300 ratings began work at Kerry Road alongside ratings from the TAMY.

Rear Admiral Portal, the FONAP, carried out an inspection on 22 October after which he told the ship's company that MONAB 7 was to be demobilised with most of the personnel being transferred to HMS *Nabsford*, the TAMY. The transfer was carried out soon afterwards and MONAB 7 paid off on 5 November 1945 with most of the personnel continuing to work in the TAMY complex while they awaited demobilisation.

MONAB 7 sources:

• Report on the Organisation of the Flag Officer Naval Air Pacific in the Archive of the Fleet Air Arm Museum.
• *www.faahistoryweb*

Chapter Fifteen

MONAB 8

HMS Nabcatcher
RNAS Kai Tak

The personnel of MONAB 8 began to assemble at RNAS Middle Wallop in May 1945. It differed from earlier MONABs in that it was only intended to support fighter aircraft and was issued appropriate tools and spares. The technical components included MM 7, MS 13, MS 14 and MSR 9. Between them they were expected to support Seafires, Corsairs and Fireflies.

At last, there was sufficient feedback to allow a practical element in the unit's training and MONAB 8 was the first to able to set up a mobile base that gave the sailors some familiarity with the equipment they were expected to use operationally. It was established at Cranford, near Middle Wallop and involved 12 officers and 110 ratings who set up tents, Dorland hangars and mobile workshops. With the end of the war in Europe, greater emphasis could be given to the delivery of vehicles on time and the cataloguing of stores with the result that this unit was probably the best prepared before it left the UK. MONAB 8 commissioned

as an independent unit, carrying its own accounts, as HMS *Nabcatcher* on 1 July 1945 under Captain V N Surtees DSO RN.

Personnel and vehicles travelled to Liverpool on 5 July. The former embarked in the troopship RMS *Maloja* and the latter, together with the stores, in SS *Empire Chieftain*. There was no need to sail in convoy and this MONAB was the first to sail for Australia eastwards through the Mediterranean Sea and the Suez Canal. Both ships sailed on 7 July 1945.

Maloja arrived in Sydney on 31 August 1945, after the war had ended and personnel moved into the tented accommodation at Warwick Farm Racecourse. With the sudden end of hostilities, however, there was no requirement for MONAB 8 in Australia and the BPF decided to deploy it to Hong Kong to take over the newly liberated airfield at Kai Tak. An advance party embarked in HMS *Slinger* on 5 September and the remainder embarked in HMS *Reaper* later in the month. The MONAB took over the western half of the

Corsairs of 1850 NAS disembarked from HMS Vengeance to RNAS Kai Tak in October 1945.

airfield and set up its mobile equipment. It re-commissioned as HMS *Nabcatcher* at RNAS Kai Tak on 26 September 1945. The RAF also planned to use the airfield and it became a joint venture with the RAF responsible for air traffic control arrangements. MONAB 8 provided facilities for squadrons disembarked from carriers and a base for a Fleet Requirements Unit (FRU).

Japanese POWs were used as working parties at Kai Tak for some months after the war. They mustered on the Quarterdeck every morning and bowed to the white ensign as a mark of respect. A typhoon was an early setback. It blew down a number of tents and ripped the cover off a Dorland hangar, which was never found! Aircraft operations started with the disembarkation of 1701 NAS Sea Otters from *Vengeance* on 3 October and 1846 NAS Corsairs from *Colossus* on 12 October. They were followed by 1850 NAS Corsairs from *Vengeance* and 827 Barracudas

from *Colossus*. They re-embarked in their carriers from 18 October onwards. 721 NAS was disembarked from *Speaker* on 11 January 1946 to become the resident FRU. Another typhoon caused extensive damage to aircraft in July 1946.

MONAB 8 ceased to exist on paper on 27 August 1946 when its accounts were transferred to HMS *Tamar* the RN Barracks. The Name Nabcatcher was retained to describe the RN Air Section at RAF Kai Tak until it finally paid off on 1 April 1947. The Section re-commissioned on the same day as HMS *Flycatcher*, the name formerly used by the MONAB base in the UK. The renamed section remained a tender to HMS *Tamar* until it, too, paid off on 31 December 1947 when the naval facility was reduced to 'Care & Maintenance' status. It was never re-opened although the airfield continued in use as an RAF establishment for many years.

MONAB 8 sources:

- Report on the Organisation of the Flag Officer Naval Air Pacific in the Archive of the Fleet Air Arm Museum.
- The Squadrons of the Fleet Air Arm by Ray Sturtivant & Theo Balance. Published by Air Britain in 1994.
- *www.faahistoryweb*

Chapter Sixteen

MONAB 9

HMS Nabrock
RNAS Sembawang

Like the previous unit, MONAB 9 was intended to support disembarked fighter squadrons in the BPF. Its purpose emphasised the fact that fighters had, by 1945, eclipsed other types of embarked aircraft and they represented the majority of fleet units. Personnel began to assemble at RNAS Middle Wallop on 1 July 1945. As a result of another lesson learnt, heavy equipment and bulk stores were dispatched to the Far East ahead of the personnel on 20 July. It was originally to have been named *Nabsmere* but this was changed before the process of forming up was complete. Technical components included MM 8, MS 15 and MS 16 capable of supporting Seafires, Corsairs and Hellcats.

MONAB 9 commissioned as an independent command with its own accounts at RNAS Middle Wallop on 1 August 1945 under Captain J S C Salter OBE DSC RN. The end of the war led the Admiralty to delay the unit's departure and a number of men were sent on leave on VJ Day while its future was considered. It was decided to deploy MONAB 9, making it the last to deploy to Australia. Personnel embarked in MV *Dominion Monarch* in Liverpool with the remaining light stores and sailed on 30 August 1945. There was no need for convoy and the ship took passage through the Mediterranean Sea and the Indian Ocean, calling at Auckland and Christchurch, New Zealand before docking in Sydney. Once there the ratings moved into the tented accommodation at Warwick Farm Racecourse while plans were made to deploy the unit to Singapore. The decision to use

MONAB 9 to take over the recently liberated airfield at Sembawang in Singapore had been taken in time to divert the ship carrying the heavy equipment and stores directly to Singapore. A series of three advance parties were flown from Australia to Singapore by RAF transport aircraft. The main party followed in MV *Largs Bay*, an aged Australian troopship.

The advance party re-commissioned HMS *Nabrock* at RNAS Sembawang on 5 October 1945. The airfield had been left in a bad state by the Japanese and was littered with damaged aircraft and other debris. The main party landed from *Largs Bay* on 1 November and was employed at first to make the airfield and living accommodation useable. After that they assembled crated American aircraft, mainly Hellcats, so that they were more manageable. When on their wheels, they were loaded onto aircraft carriers, taken out to sea and ditched over the side since the Lend/Lease agreement with the USA stipulated that aircraft must be paid for or destroyed at the end of hostilities.

MONAB 9 ended its brief existence on 15 December 1945 when Nabrock paid off at Sembawang. The air station was re-commissioned on the same day as HMS *Simbang*, RNAS Sembawang, retaining many of the MONAB's personnel. Many of the vehicles and much of the MONAB equipment were retained, however, supplemented by equipment transported to Singapore from disbanded MONABs in Australia. Both vehicles and equipment were maintained in reserve until the 1950s but never, in fact, used.

MONAB 9 sources:

- Report on the Organisation of the Flag Officer Naval Air Pacific in the Archive of the Fleet Air Arm Museum.
- DNAT Newsletter.
- CB 03164 Progress in Naval Aviation – Summary Number 1 for the period ending 1 December 1947.
- *www.faahistoryweb*

Chapter Seventeen

MONAB 10

HMS Nabhurst
Held in reserve at: RNAS Lossiemouth
RNAS Henstridge

The last MONAB to commission as an independent command with its own accounts began to assemble at RNAS Middle Wallop in July 1945. It commissioned on 1 September 1945 with Commander T S Jackson in command but, with the end of the war, there was no longer an operational requirement for the unit. The Admiralty decided to retain it in reduced form, however, to act as a trials and development unit within the MNAO to keep the art alive. This new role did not require it to be an autonomous unit, though and it paid off on 12 October 1945, personnel being borne on the books of HMS *Flycatcher* from that date. The technical components retained were MM 9, MS 17, MS 18 and MR 4. They were originally intended to support fighters but with the adoption of the trial role, they had to be capable of supporting a more general range of types.

When RNAS Middle Wallop was closed, *Flycatcher* paid off on 10 April 1946 and MONAB 10 was split between three different sites - RNAS Fearn, RNAS Inskip and RNAE Risley pending the handover of Lossiemouth from the RAF to the Navy. The MNAO and MONAB 10 actually moved into Lossiemouth during May and June, while the station was still under RAF control, with the exception of the radio and radar vans which went into storage elsewhere. RNAS Lossiemouth commissioned on 12 July 1946 and its extensive storage hangars were used for both reserve aircraft and the MNAO's equipment.

MR 4 was used to support aircraft operating from Lossiemouth's satellite airfield at RNAS Milltown.

In 1951 it was decided to re-vitalise MONAB 10 with a possible role in the Korean War. The unit was to move to a 'mothballed' air station at Henstridge in Dorset and was fully installed by the end of 1952. The personnel were borne on the books of the nearby RNAS Yeovilton and accommodated there. The unit underwent several improvements including the establishment of an aircraft depreservation section, but continued to lead a low profile existence with no flying operations. Henstridge itself was run on a 'care and maintenance' basis at three months notice to resume operations. The MNAO used the buildings and hangars but the airfield itself was returned to agricultural use. The last commanding officer was Commander M J A O'Sullivan RN who was appointed on 11 May 1954.

MONAB 10 was disbanded on 2 July 1955. Its equipment was left at Henstridge and gradually scrapped as Admiralty supplied equipment was removed from the airfield prior to its full reversion to civilian use after 1956. The Admiralty's Director of Air Operations and Training (DAOT) stated in April 1956 that the last MONAB had been dispersed and that its equipment was, in any case, obsolete. This marked the end of MONAB operations in the Royal Navy.

MONAB 10 sources:

- The Development of British Naval Aviation Volume III – unpublished manuscript in the author's collection.
- The Squadrons of the Fleet Air Arm by Ray Sturtivant & Theo Balance. Published by Air Britain in 1994.
- CB 03164 – Progress in Naval Aviation. 1951, 1952, 1954 and 1956 editions.
- Confidential Admiralty Fleet Order 139/51.
- *www.faahistoryweb*

Chapter Eighteen

CANCELLED MONABS

The Admiralty had approved plans to commission fifteen MONABs and two TAMYs. These would have been used to man the extra airfields projected for RN use in Australia in late 1945, early 1946. Only nine of the former and one of the latter had been commissioned before VJ Day on 15 August 1945, however, but steps had been taken to assemble some of the projected units. The second TAMY only ever existed as a paper plan and, given the experience with TAMY 1, might never have been proceeded with.

MONAB 11 began to assemble at RNAS Middle Wallop in August 1945 under Commander K W Beard RN. Its formation was suspended after VJ Day and, when no operational role could be found for it, it was dispersed at the end of August.

MONAB 12 was projected to form at RNAS Middle Wallop from 1 September 1945. Some personnel began to assemble in August but they were dispersed at the end of the month when it was decided not to proceed with the unit.

MONAB 13 was cancelled after the drafting process for personnel had started but before assembly at RNAS Middle Wallop was due to begin in October 1945.

MONAB 14, to have formed in November 1945, was cancelled.

MONAB 15, to have formed in December 1945, was cancelled.

TAMY 2 was projected but no steps were taken to assemble it.

Cancelled MONAB's sources:

• CB 03164 – Progress in Naval Aviation 1945 edition.
• *www.faahistoryweb*

Chapter Nineteen

ROYAL NAVY FORWARD AIRCRAFT POOL 1
USNAS Pityilu

BPF plans to set up a forward base, including airfields, at Samar in the Philippines were abandoned when it was realised that lodger facilities at US naval air facilities were too far from the fleet anchorage at Leyte Gulf and insufficient for the fleet's needs. Further, the passage for replenishment carriers to the operational areas off Japan was only marginally less than that from Manus and the haul for ferry carriers from Australia was greater. The decision was taken, therefore, to support Task Force 37 from Manus. MONAB 4 had already been established on Ponam Island with some facilities for reserve aircraft. Additionally, a small pool was maintained in *Unicorn* but a larger pool was needed at a shore base to support the large-scale operations planned for the 1st and 11th Aircraft Carrier Squadrons in the autumn of 1945. Since the US Navy had largely moved its support operations forward to Guam and the Philippines, it made lodger facilities available at its naval air station on Pityilu Island.

Pityilu is another island in the Admiralty group. It is just over 20 miles east of Ponam Island and forms part of the western, outer reef of Seeadler Harbour, which was used as the fleet anchorage. It was thus ideally placed and well equipped without the need for a fully equipped MONAB that an unmanned airfield would have required. It had been built by the SeaBees during the second half of 1944 after liberation from the Japanese and, apart from the airfield, had accommodation for several thousand sailors to be landed for rest and recreation. It was, thus, able to accommodate the new unit with ease. Both Ponam and Pityilu were about to offer relaxation facilities ashore for visiting BPF ships during their short 'lives'.

Forward Aircraft Pool Number 1 was formed in Australia in June 1945 from components removed from MONABs 1 and 2. These included MSR 1 and reflected the fact that the primary requirement in Australia was to produce aircraft and get them into the supply chain rather than store them. The unit assembled at Nowra on 7 June commanded by Lieutenant Commander (A) D A Horton RNVR and embarked in *Pioneer* for passage, leaving Sydney on 16 June 1945. It disembarked at Pityilu on 21 June 1945 and began at once to establish a pool of serviceable, operational aircraft of all types for issue to the replenishment carriers. Apart from the need to fly its own aircraft constantly to keep them serviceable, test flight teams from the maintenance carriers *Unicorn* and *Pioneer* worked ashore to test fly aircraft that had been repaired on board. The FAP held examples of all the types in use with the BPF and was operating efficiently by mid July.

When the war ended sooner than anticipated on 15 August, the need for the pool disappeared, literally overnight. BPF Headquarters gave orders that it was to close by mid-September and aircraft were flown to Ponam from where they were embarked in maintenance, replenishment and ferry carriers for passage to Australia. *Unicorn* moored off the island on 17 September to evacuate personnel and equipment to Australia, after which the lodger facilities were relinquished. The airfield continued in use by the USN until 1 September 1947.

RNFAP 1 sources:

- Report on the Organisation of the Flag Officer Naval Air Pacific in the Archive of the Fleet Air Arm Museum.
- Report on the Experience of the BPF – 1946 in the Archive of the Fleet Air Arm Museum.
- The Development of British Naval Aviation Vol III – unpublished manuscript in the Author's Collection.
- *www.faahistoryweb*

Chapter Twenty

TAMY 1

HMS Nabsford
RNAY Archerfield

The Kerry Road workshop and hangar complex with RNAS Archerfield in the background.

The TAMY was the largest element of the MNAO and proved to be the most difficult to deploy and set to work. Personnel began to assemble in December 1944 and, since both MONABs 3 and 4 were still at RNAS Ludham, there was insufficient accommodation for the large new unit. In consequence, like MONAB 2, it had to be split into two sections. The Headquarters element formed at Ludham and the technical elements formed at HMS *Gosling*, RNAE Risley. Both elements had to assist the MONAB HQ at Ludham with hands to perform routine station tasks in addition to their own

training. Both had to draw battledress and weapons in addition to collecting tools and equipment appropriate to the yard's tasks as well as carrying out short aircraft maintenance courses.

The yard's intended task was to carry out major repairs, overhauls and inspections. Secondary tasks were to carry out the erection of a limited number of aircraft and engine overhauls building up to 100 per month. With the wisdom of hindsight, these were unrealistic targets and it is difficult to see how a transportable unit, which was originally intended to work under canvas, could ever have carried them out. The

TAMY commissioned as HMS *Nabsford* on 1 February 1945 under Commander B J L Rogers-Tillstone RN.

Personnel of both MONAB 5 and the TAMY travelled to the Gladstone Docks in Liverpool by road and rail on 16 February. The air yard's main party comprised 23 officers and 1,191 ratings and they embarked in SS *Stirling Castle*, sailing for Australia on 18 February. A second party, comprising 8 officers and 91 ratings, sailed in SS *Empress of Scotland* on 10 March. Stores, vehicles and equipment sailed in two groups, the first sailing from Liverpool in SS *Empire Waimana* on 20 February and the second in SS *Hororata* on 1 March. An advance party of 4 officers and 28 ratings flew ahead to Australia in order to make early arrangements to move into the Archerfield complex ten miles south of Brisbane which had been

selected as the initial site for the air yard. *Stirling Castle* landed personnel for the TAMY at Brisbane on 27 March and then sailed for Sydney to land the personnel of MONAB 5.

The advance party arrived in Brisbane in February and was augmented by a party of 80 sailors from the RN Barracks in Sydney that helped to take over former US Navy accommodation at Rocklea Camp. By then, the US personnel had moved on to new bases in the Philippines. The advance party was also tasked with erecting 16 Corsairs at Kerry Road, Archerfield. They lacked equipment, spare parts and tools but managed to complete 12 before the main body arrived on 27 March, with the help of the RAAF, the Department of Aircraft Production and local engineering firms with knowledge of aviation work. Rocklea Camp became the administrative and accommodation centre

The Rocklea plant.

The facility for ground running aircraft engines

of the air yard but the air yard grew rapidly to absorb many other facilities that were several miles apart. In addition to the camp, the air yard was eventually to expand to include an airfield at Archerfield and erection, inspection, repair, radio and gunnery workshops at Kerry Road. Engine and ancillary workshops were at Rocklea Factory and facilities for the dismantling of airframes and engines for spare parts were established at Benedict Stone Works. Stores and spare parts were held at Runcorn.

Despite the arrival of the main party, aircraft erection remained slow because large numbers of sailors were miss-employed converting the accommodation to RN standards, dismantling the single beds and fitted wardrobes left by the USN to install the two-tier bunks brought out from the UK. They also had to fit out offices and other administrative facilities before the TAMY could begin to function effectively.

The use of such widely dispersed facilities led to a significant requirement for transport. A number of vehicles were lent to the unit by the Australian Department of Aircraft Production, including several 100 seat buses which ferried sailors between their accommodation, the various workshops and the main dining hall which was in Rocklea Factory, half a mile from the camp. The trucks sent out from the UK would not have been as effective and did not, in any case, arrive for several weeks after the TAMY started work.

The scale of the task that the TAMY was expected to perform was daunting. While it struggled to create the infrastructure to carry out its work, it still lacked ground equipment, tools and stores that had not yet arrived in Australia in their slow transport ships. Everything that was used had to be borrowed from the RAAF or manufactured under local contract by

A view of the accommodation area at TAMY 1 taken over from the United States' Seabees.

Australian engineering firms in the Brisbane area. The lack of spare parts defeated plans to overhaul 100 engines a month and that figure was never achieved. The need to create new works was beyond the capacity of the Allied Works Council and sailors had to be employed to build and fit out new workshops and gun butts. Despite the size of the establishment, the TAMY never had a sick bay or dental department and had to rely on facilities at other service establishments in the Brisbane area throughout the remainder of the war. Undaunted by the enormity of the task ahead of it, TAMY 1 re-commissioned as HMS ***Nabsford***, RNAY Archerfield on 27 March 1945, the day the main party arrived at the complex.

Significant aircraft production got into its stride in April. The planned output for its first month of operation was:

15 major inspections
25 minor inspections and modifications
25 aircraft erections
25 engine overhauls
component repairs arising from the above

The achievement was 4 Corsairs erected with assistance given to a firm in Archerfield that erected 3 Expediters. An air-to-sea firing range was built up in Moreton bay for general use by BPF aircraft.

The programme and achievement for May were:

Programme	Performance
Erections	
15 Seafires	9 Seafire
35 Corsairs	15 Corsairs
Minor Inspections	
7 Corsairs	7 Corsairs

Shortages of workshop equipment and spares were the chief reasons why only half the erection programme was completed. As a consequence, the TAMY decided to change the balance of manpower allocation, taking sailors off the longer term construction projects and re-allocating them to improve, as much as possible, the output of aircraft for the fleet. A staged system of erection was introduced, following the technique pioneered at Bankstown by MONAB 2. The required monthly output was increased from 25 to 75 erections while the number of inspections remained as before. A new function, the reduction of badly damaged aircraft from the front line to spares and produce was added. New premises at Benedict Stone Works were taken over for this task. These were about seven miles from Rocklea Camp, adding significantly to the transport problem but they were close to the jetties where the aircraft would be landed. The yard's MT section was expanded as a consequence.

For June the programme and achievement were:

Programme	Performance
Erections	
10 Seafires	Nil
40 Corsairs	24 Corsairs
Minor inspections	
14 Corsairs	6 Corsairs

The failure to erect any Seafires was due to none being available until the end of the month. Corsair production was afflicted by the need to change 11 engines that had been contaminated by sand and the lack of Type SCR 522 connectors. The minor inspections were slowed by the need to rectify the considerable corrosion, which the aircraft had suffered in transit. The Runcorn stores depot was taken over during this month, obviating the need to build a new 20,000 square foot store at Kerry Road. Whilst this was good news, it was six miles from Rocklea Camp and four from Kerry Road, adding still further to the need for transport. Critically, the new facility provided enough storage for the vast quantities of air stores and equipment that were beginning to arrive in Australia for the TAMY and without it, they would have had to be left in their crates in the open.

Although it was not known at the time, July was to be the last full month requiring wartime production schedules. Programme and performance were:

Programme	Performance
Erections	
All available Seafires (up to 25)	9 Seafires
25 Corsairs	23 Corsairs
Minor Inspections	
15 Corsairs	11 Corsairs
	1 engine change
	1 Avenger major inspection

A bad delay in Seafire production was caused by a batch being received with unmatched mainplanes. The shortfall in Corsairs was due to shortages of spare parts. The ability to carry out test flights at Archerfield airfield was improved during this month by the completion of a maintenance test facility manned by ground crew who were expert in curing test flying 'snags' under the leadership of the senior test pilot. The vast quantities of stores arriving at Runcorn led to

a request for a big increase in the number of supply ratings in order to cope with them. On 1 July the commanding officer was promoted to captain and on 8 July rear Admiral Portal, the FONAP, carried out an Inspection of the establishment. In an attempt to improve Seafire production, a small detachment from the TAMY, supplemented by men from MONAB 7 set up a Seafire erection facility at RAAF Oakey. To round off a varied month, *Nabsford* held a ship's company dance in Brisbane City Hall on 28 July 1945.

Programme and performance for August were:

Programme	Performance
Erections	
25 Seafires	9 Seafires
40 Corsairs	23 Corsairs
Inspections	
15 Corsairs	1 Corsair
	1 Seafire

After five months of operation, these were poor results, partially explained by the lack of urgency felt by many sailors after the VJ Day celebrations. Corsair production had suffered from the requirement to fit them with newly supplied gyro gun sights and to comply with a Signal Instruction which required a great deal of work to get at their fuel control valves. 300 ratings of MONAB 7 started work at Kerry Road early in the month. Although they obviously had the potential to increase output, they took time to learn the system of erection in use and were not fully efficient by the time the war ended.

No mention of engine overhaul has been included in the performance figures for the very good reason that none was carried out until the necessary quantities of stores arrived in September. By then, however, the BPF's requirement for replacement equipment had reduced considerably and effort began to be put into stripping airframes and preparing Lend/Lease aircraft for ditching at sea.

On 15 October 721 NAS was disembarked from *Unicorn* having been withdrawn from RNAS Ponam. The unit was re-equipped with new aircraft for service in Hong Kong with MONAB 8 at Kai Tak but spent some weeks at Archerfield preparing for its new role. Its establishment included Defiant target tugs, Corsairs, Avengers and a Harvard. Sea Otters of 1701 NAS also moved in from Maryborough en route to Hong Kong. They deployed in *Striker* in early November and 721 deployed in *Speaker* on 28 December.

FONAP returned on 22 October and cleared lower deck to tell the ship's company that there was a continuing role for an air yard in support of the BPF but that it would be gradually reduced in size. The combined TAMY/MONAB 7 had a ship's company of just over 2,000 at the time. 500 sailors from the TAMY were released to return to the UK in SS *Strathenden* in late October and MONAB 7 paid off on 5 November 1945. Some of its people moved to the TAMY, some to *Golden Hind* and others returned to the UK for demobilisation.

In February 1946 the TAMY began to run down with 1,000 men being sent back to the UK via the barracks in Sydney. The remainder set about closing down the component establishments and handing them back to the Australian authorities. The vast stockpiles of stores and equipment had to be returned or destroyed. HMS *Nabsford*, RNAY Archerfield paid off on 31 March 1946.

More than any other component of the MNAO, the TAMY came in for considerable scrutiny after the war. Unlike the MONABs that were intended to fulfil specific tasks, the air yard was a large and complex industrial organisation that was allowed insufficient time to mature. It could never, really, have been transportable and was hampered by the lack of a nucleus of officers and men skilled in aircraft maintenance and repair work. The TAMY lacked facilities on the ground, equipment, stores and the necessary skills with the result that the advance party was called upon to carry a crushing burden of preparation. Further, aircraft repair was a non-standardised discipline unlike the erection of new aircraft and needed skills that were in short supply in the newly formed and hastily trained

unit. Very few damaged aircraft were brought back from the fleet and the FAMG repair facilities were never stretched. The TAMY found itself acting as a RDU, concentrating on erection rather than inspection; a task originally thought to be of secondary importance for it.

In his 'haul-down' report, the FONAP expressed the opinion that the expenditure of energy, manpower and material in starting the air yard had not been justified. Air stores, ground equipment and skilled sailors were the 'life-blood' of deep maintenance and repair. They should have been in place in Australia before attempting to establish the air yard. Further, the complexity of aircraft by 1945 made it essential to have units that specialised in work on a single type. A number of specialised MR components with access to suitable workshops like those taken over at Bankstown would have been a more effective use of resources. In summary, he considered the TAMY a development that was not worth repeating.

The Seafire erection line in hangar M27 in TAMY 1.

TAMY 1 sources:

- Report on the Organisation of the Flag Officer Naval Air Pacific in the Archive of the Fleet Air Arm Museum.
- Report of the Experience of the British Pacific Fleet – 1946 in the Archive of the Fleet Air Arm Museum.
- The Development of British Naval Aviation Vol III – Unpublished manuscript in the Author's Collection.
- The Fleet Train by David Brown – Part of the British Pacific & East Indies Fleet "Forgotten Fleets" 50th Anniversary Publication 1995.

- The Forgotten Bases: The Royal Navies in the Pacific by David Brown. Part of The Royal Australian Navy in World War 2, second edition, edited by David Stevens. Published by Allen & Unwin, Crows Nest NSW in 2005.

Chapter Twenty One

AFTER 1945

With the end of a global war there was no longer a need to maintain an aircraft support organisation on such a large scale. The MONABs decreased in size and evolved, in some cases, into permanent air stations that saw service with the post-war navy. Nowra and Bankstown became RAN establishments. The immediate peace-time tasks were to reduce the scale of the fleet's activities, demobilise manpower and to hand the majority of the bases back to their former owners. The majority of the Royal Navy's aircraft were Lend/Lease types and the rules under which they had been borrowed called for them to be purchased, returned to the USA or destroyed at the end of hostilities. The latter was the cheapest option and literally thousands of aircraft were dumped at sea across the world, 740 of them off the east coast of Australia. These included not only the front-line types such as the Corsair, Hellcat and

Avenger but second-line aircraft such as the Vengeance. Aircraft with a potential commercial use such as the Expediter and Reliant had to be returned, intact, to the USA where a significant number still exist. British types such as the Barracuda were not exempt. They were available in larger numbers in the UK than the peace-time fleet needed and so many of these also found their way to a watery 'grave'. Engines, spare parts and even ammunition also went over the side into the sea.

By 1946, the decision was taken centralise the receipt and storage of all naval aircraft at air stations in the UK although small numbers to support deployed fleets were to be kept at air stations in Malta and Singapore. These were held by Naval Aircraft Storage Units (NASU) which contained both maintenance personnel and pilots to keep some aircraft in flying condition as operational reserves. Most of these originat-

*A Grumman Avenger being pushed over the bow of **HMS Pioneer**. Note the white lines painted on the deck to align the aircraft wheels. The holes hacked in the aircraft structure were to ensure that it sank quickly.*

*An Avenger being ditched from **Implacable** in May 1946.*

ed in RN establishments but moved into RAF bases such when the size of the task decreased to the point where retention of a fully manned RN air station was no longer viable. Examples included Changi in Singapore, Muharraq in Bahrain and RAAF Iwakuni in Japan. Changi, the last of these closed in 1971.

The RFA continued to operate Air Stores Issuing Ships and **Reliant** was fitted out in the 1950s to support fast carrier task forces. By the mid 1970s air stores were re-organised on joint service lines, after the Templer Committee's Report, and the RAF took responsibility for all fixed-wing aircraft support and the RN for all rotary-wing. Spare parts were held in centralised depots in the UK and flown by commercial aircraft to anywhere they were needed quickly. The contemporary rise in the number of flights to global destinations made this a practical scheme in peace-time. For particularly difficult repair, modification or

survey work, members of a Mobile Aircraft Repair Transport and Salvage Unit (MARTSU) could be flown to support embarked squadron personnel using either commercial or RAF transport depending on the size of the task. Despite relying on 'postal' or air transport support, carriers could remain at sea for an indefinite period using their Carrier-on-board Delivery (COD) Gannet or, with the advent of the Sea King after 1970, helicopters to ferry spares and passengers out to the ship.

The system was severely tested in 1982 during the South Atlantic Conflict when consideration was given to re-commissioning the light fleet carrier **Bulwark** as an aircraft maintenance carrier. In the event, the proposal was not taken forward. This was partially because of the poor material state of the ship; she might have had to be towed to the Falklands. The main cause, however, was the fact that the only avail-

able machine tools and equipment to fulfil the task were in use at the RN Air Yards at Fleetlands and Perth supporting UK helicopters throughout the world. If it had been moved onto the ship, **Bulwark** would have had to take on the whole task because the stripped-out air yards could no longer function. This was clearly impractical and the existing system, imperfect as it might be, had to be made to work by the Naval Aircraft Repair Organisation (NARO) ashore. The problem provides an interesting contrast with the relatively straightforward equipping of the MONABs in addition to dozens of air yards and air stations less than thirty years previously. In the 1990s the NARO was replaced by a defence agency, the Defence Aircraft Repair Agency (DARA) which took over the running of Fleetlands, Perth and the RAF air yard at St Athan in Wales. In 2006 it appears that the agency will, in

turn, be at least partially sold to commercial interests as the total number of UK military aircraft continues to decline.

Only **Unicorn**, of all the wartime maintenance ships, saw any further service in anything like her designed role after 1945. **Pioneer** saw no further service and **Perseus** spent a brief period as a trials ship and ferry carrier but their half sister **Triumph** was converted into a fleet maintenance ship between 1957 and 1964. In her new guise, she contained limited facilities for the support of Wasp helicopters from Leander and Tribal class frigates as they underwent maintenance. A small hangar and 'helipad' were built onto the former flight deck for them since the original hangar had been converted into workshops. With an extension built to port of the island and her sponsons removed, the rebuilt **Triumph** bore a close resemblance to

*A variety of aircraft on the flightdeck of **Pioneer** for transport to the UK. They include a Beech Expiditor (minus wings), together with Seafires, Fireflies and a Harvard.*

Perseus and *Pioneer*. She spent some years in the Far East Fleet before returning to the UK in 1972 to pay off into reserve at Chatham. She was towed away to be scrapped in Spain shortly before the Falklands War, a sad waste of a valuable asset.

The most recognisable legacy of the MONAB organisation is the Royal Navy's Commando Helicopter Force, home based at RNAS Yeovilton. The four helicopter squadrons provide essential mobility for the Royal Marines' 3 Commando Brigade and are equally capable of operating in ships, such as the commando carrier Ocean, or ashore in Forward Operating Bases (FOB). To help them achieve this, the force includes a support element which includes catering, medical facilities and assault engineers. The latter are capable of clearing landing sites, creating bulk fuel installations and enabling technical support for helicopters in tented hangars. The whole force has to be capable of deploying at short notice to temperate, jungle, desert or arctic locations and must be equally at home in all of them. Alternatively, detachments might be deployed concurrently in many locations such as the Middle East, Northern Norway and West Africa. Each would have an element of the support force. Within this support cell, there are several Mobile Air Operations Teams (MAOT) equipped with sophisticated communications built into all-terrain vehicles. They are responsible for marking out landing sites and for providing air traffic control for assault helicopter operations.

The Commando Helicopter Force has evolved since the first commando squadron commissioned in 1960 and is now commanded by a Captain RN. It regularly deploys as part of national, UN, NATO and other coalition force elements.

As joint forces become the normal method of deployment, joint support, command and control organisations have gradually taken over from single-service formations. By 2006 all fixed-wing operations are controlled by Joint Force Air Component Headquarters (JFAC HQ) and similar arrangements will, no doubt, extend to helicopter operations. JFACs have taken control of operations both ashore and afloat now that the aircraft carriers *Illustrious* and *Ark Royal* have been converted into the strike role. No matter what form future support and command arrangements might take, however, they will owe much to the legacy of the maintenance carriers, MONABs and the TAMY described in these pages.

SCHEME OF COMPLEMENT FOR A TYPICAL MONAB

Component	Function	Officers	SR	JR	Total
A	Executive	11	21	117	149
C	Medical	4	1	8	13
S	Stores	2	3	28	33
F	Flying control	10	1	35	46
R	Radio and radar	4	10	49	63
MG	Maintenance gunnery	3	7	45	55
MS	Maintenance servicing	4	16	10	30
MM	Mobile maintenance	6	25	64	85
MATMU	Torpedo maintenance	1	2	30	33
Total					**507**

In addition to the tented accommodation for the MONAB's own personnel, its mobile facilities were expected to house and feed disembarked squadrons up to a total of 140 officers, 125 senior rates and 665 juniors rates, a grand total of 950.

MONABs that were intended to hold reserve aircraft in large numbers had a Mobile Storage and Reserve (MSR) Component attached to them. These typically comprised 3 officers, 20 senior rates and 99 junior rates, a total of 122.

In practice no two MONABs had the same ship's company as each was modified to meet specific tasks. MONAB 7 was probably the closest approximation to a "standard" complement.

Appendix 1 sources:

• Report on the Organisation of the Flag Officer Naval Air Pacific in the Archive of the Fleet Air Arm

VEHICLES ISSUED TO A TYPICAL MONAB

Prime Movers	Number
Jeeps	12
Lorries, 3-ton, general service	34
Lorry, aircraft machine shop	1
Lorry, general workshop	1
Lorry, battery charging	1
Lorry, 22kw Lister generator	4
Lorry, refuelling bowser	4
Lorry, breakdown	1
Lorry, camp lighting equipment	6
Lorry, aerial tuning	1
Lorry, aerial transmitting	1
Lorry, IFF transmit/receive	1
Lorry, 15kw alternator	2
Lorry, diesel tanker	1
Lorry, tipping	2
Lorry, photographic equipment tender	1
Lorry, flying control vehicle	1
Lorry, 10 wheel VHF/DF	1
Lorry, mobile sick bay dispensary	1
Crash tender	2
Ambulance	2
Crane, Coles	1
Lorry, water purification plant	1
Bulldozer, tracked	1
Tractor, articulated	1
Tractors, Fordson industrial	4
Tractor, Matador, mobile laundry	1

Trailers	
Trailer, jeep	12
Trailer, water carrier, 150 gallon	5
Trailer, office	1
Trailer, mobile laundry	1
Trailer, pump	2
Trailer, generator for photographic tender	1
Trailer. high power	6
Trailer, medium power	2
Trailer, generator for VHF/DF lorry	1

Prime Movers	Number
Trailer, floodlighting	1
Trailer, landmark beacon (pundit)	1
Trailer, M/T servicing	1
Trailer, NAAFI refreshments	1
Trailer, mobile bakery, 7 ton	1
Total number of vehicles	130

POST HOSTILITIES

After the end of hostilities, both the BPF and the logistic support required to keep it at sea were analysed extensively. Many changes to the composition of the post war fleet came about as a result and two of the recommendations summarized below are relevant to this work.

The balanced fleet and its air train.

Although the operational object of a fleet may be clear, and the most suitable composition of types to fulfill this object easily arrived at, its actual size and composition, and its ability to remain at sea in the operational area, will be dependant on the following factors:

- Facilities and resources at the main base.
- Facilities available at any advanced base.
- Distance between main and advanced bases.
- Distance between advanced base, bulk fuel terminal and fleet sea replenishment positions.
- Shipping available to provide the fleet with fuel, aircraft, ammunition etc in the replenishment areas.

It may be any one of these factors alone which could limit the size or composition of a fleet or its operational capability. To neglect these points, or fail to give due consideration to them, may mean hamstringing a fleet and seriously curtailing its operations.

During Operation ICEBERG no major failure in the supply of aircraft occurred but there was never a safe margin. Had losses been heavier, it might have led to the curtailment of operations by the RN. In the July/August operations against the Japanese mainland, the fuelling area was frequently changed by 3rd Fleet by as much as 500 miles due to weather and other operational causes. With no margin of spare tankers, a very serious situation was developing when the end of the war solved the problem. Even so, it was necessary for some of our ships to refuel from USN tankers.

The ideal replenishment carrier

Should such a type be required again, it must be a fully efficient operational carrier and not treated as a floating reserve of personnel and stores to meet the losses of the fleet carriers. It would need a suitable catapult to fly off all types of naval aircraft in nil wind conditions. Ideally, it should have a wide range of air stores for all types of operational aircraft and a range of armament stores. Workshops should have test equipment for radio and radar and there must be at least two slings for each type of aircraft, tested and in date. A range of aircraft spare gear would be desirable but not if it had to be carried at the expense of air stores.

The replenishment carrier must be capable of transferring stores at sea without using the flight deck and have a boom to which aircraft lighters could be firmly secured while aircraft are craned onto and off them. The ship must have at least one crane with a safe working load greater than the heaviest operational aircraft. Boats must be suitable for extended operations in exposed, rough anchorages.

With regard to manning, each ship was recommended to have a standardised air maintenance party in addition

to the personnel needed to operate the flight deck. Some escort carriers had been manned by T 124X personnel on loan from the Merchant Navy. In practice these gave rise to considerable administrative problems and the arrangement was found to be a source of continuous grievance on the one side or the other. It was decided that this was always likely to be the case if certain officers and men were required to do the same work but under different conditions of pay. Such an arrangement was not believed to be suited to the requirements of replenishment carriers and, if possible, was to be avoided in future.

Appendix 3 sources:

• Report of Experience of the British Pacific Fleet 1946 in the Author's Archive

GLOSSARY

(A)	Air Branch (designation after rank).
ACCC	Australian Civilian Construction Corps.
ACS 1	Flag Officer Commanding 1st Aircraft Carrier Squadron.
1 ACS	1st Aircraft Carrier Squadron.
ACS 11	Flag Officer Commanding 11th Aircraft Carrier squadron.
11 ACS	11th Aircraft carrier squadron.
ACS 30	Commodore Commanding 30th Aircraft carrier Squadron.
30 ACS	30th Aircraft Carrier Squadron.
AD	Assistant Director.
AEO	Air Engineering Officer.
AHU	Aircraft Holding Unit.
ARS	Airframe Repair Shop.
ASIS	Air Stores Issuing Ship.
BPF	British Pacific Fleet.
C-in-C BPF	Commander-in-Chief British Pacific Fleet.
CAP	Combat Air Patrol.
CASU	Carrier Aircraft Servicing Unit.
COMAIR Pacific	Commander Air pacific (USN).
COMAT	Commodore Air Train.
COMNAS	Commodore Naval Air Stations.
CVE	Escort Aircraft Carrier.
DLT	Deck Landing Training
ERS	Engine Repair Shop.
FAE	Front Line Aircraft Establishment.
FAMG	Fleet Aircraft Maintenance Group.
FAP	Forward Aircraft Pool.
FEF	Far East Fleet.
FFO	Furnace Fuel Oil.
FONAP	Flag Officer Naval Air Pacific.
FONAS (A)	Flag Officer Naval Air Stations (Pacific).
FRU	Fleet Requirements Unit.
JASS	Joint Anti-Submarine School.
MAR	Mobile Air Radio Maintenance Component.
MATMU	Mobile Air Torpedo Maintenance Unit.

MDAP	Mutual Defence Assistance Programme.
MONAB	Mobile Operational Naval Air Base.
MNAO	Mobile Naval Airfield Organisation.
MP	Mobile Personnel Component.
MR	Mobile Repair Component.
MS	Mobile Servicing Component.
MSM	Mobile Servicing and Maintenance Component.
MSR	Mobile Servicing and Repair Component.
MT	Motor Transport.
MM	Mobile Maintenance Component.
NARO	Naval Aircraft Repair Organisation.
NARR	Naval Air radio Repair Component.
NAS	Naval Air Squadron
NASU	Naval Aircraft Salvage Unit.
NOTU	Naval Operational Training Unit.
(P)	Pilot (Qualification shown in Navy List).
RAAC	Rear Admiral Aircraft Carriers.
RAAF	Royal Australian Air Force.
RAAFVR	Royal Australian Air Force Volunteer Reserve.
RAF	Royal Air Force.
RAFT	Rear Admiral Fleet Train.
RAN	Royal Australian Navy.
RANAS	Royal Australian Naval Air Station.
RANVR	Royal Australian Naval Volunteer Reserve.
RA (Q)	Rear Admiral Logistic Support BPF.
RAS	Replenishment at Sea.
RDU	Receipt and Despatch Unit.
RFA	Royal Fleet Auxiliary.
RFAS	Royal Fleet Auxiliary Service.
RMEU	Royal Marines Engineering Unit.
RN	Royal Navy.
RNAE	Royal Naval Air Establishment.
RNAS	Royal Naval Air Station.
RNAY	Royal Naval Air Yard.
ROP	Report of Proceedings.
SAM	School of Aircraft Maintenance.
SNSO	Superintending Naval Stores Officer.
SMP	Specialist Maintenance Party.
SRP	Specialist Repair Party.
TAMY	Transportable Aircraft Maintenance Yard

TMO	Transport and Movement Office (RAAF).
USN	United States Navy.
VA (Q)	Vice Admiral Logistic Support BPF.
WRNS	Women's Royal Naval Service.